African American Homeownership Initiative

Volume 2

Eric Lawrence Frazier MBA

Your Trusted Advisor in Business and Wealth

African American Homeownership Initiative

Dedication

To every African American family who has dreamed of homeownership, faced barriers, and yet continues to push forward. This book is for you — and for the generations to come who will walk through doors that once stood closed.

ERIC LAWRENCE FRAZIER, MBA BUSINESS BOOKS

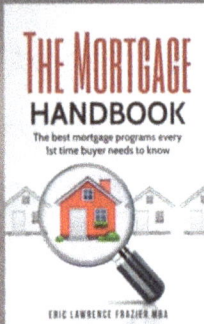

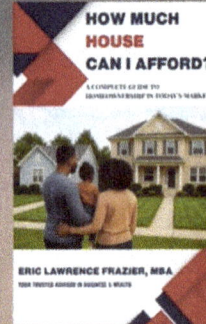

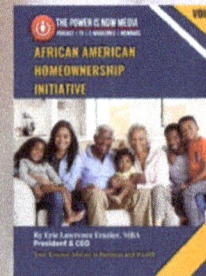

ERIC LAWRENCE FRAZIER, MBA POETRY BOOKS

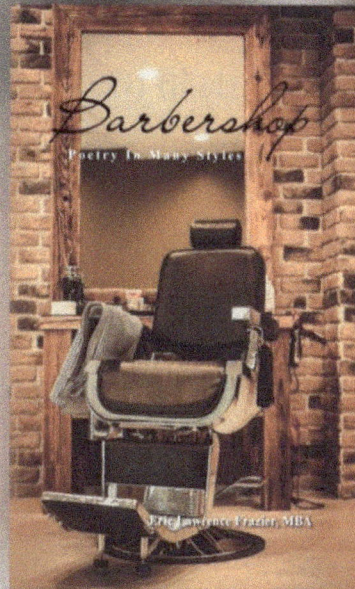

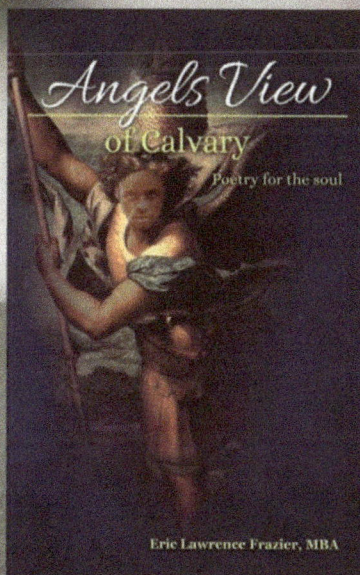

Ice Cream
Poetry In Many Flavors
Eric Lawrence Frazier, MBA

Barbershop
Poetry In Many Styles
Eric Lawrence Frazier, MBA

Angels View
of Calvary
Poetry for the soul
Eric Lawrence Frazier, MBA

TABLE OF CONTENTS

Preface

This book was born out of both frustration and determination. Frustration that, after decades of civil rights victories and policy efforts, the Black homeownership gap remains stubbornly wide. Determination because change is not only possible but necessary.

The African American Homeownership Initiative lays out the evidence, history, and contemporary realities of housing inequality in America. More importantly, it offers strategies — practical, systemic, and community-driven — to break cycles of exclusion and create sustainable opportunities for wealth building.

The chapters that follow will take you through the key barriers: financial literacy gaps, wage and wealth disparities, mortgage discrimination, and limited access to information. They also introduce solutions built on the principles of **Depower, Demystify, and Develop.**

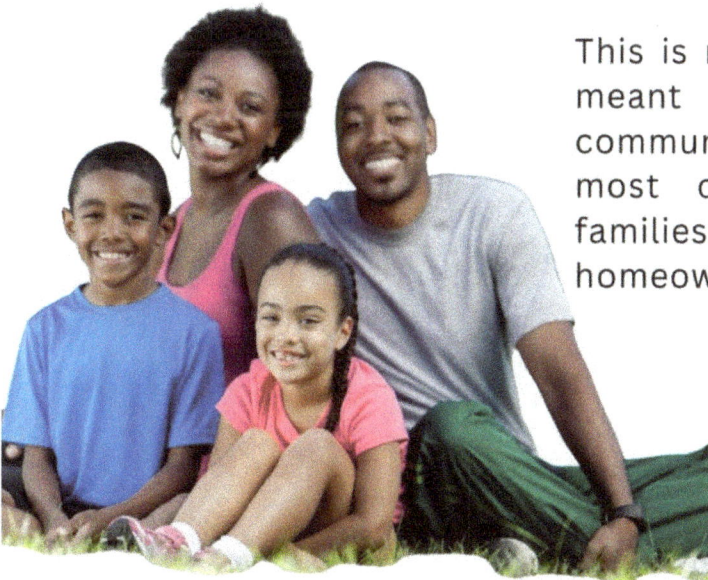

This is not just an academic text. It is meant to be used by policymakers, community leaders, educators, and most of all, by African American families navigating the path toward homeownership.

Acknowledgments

This book would not have been possible without the encouragement, contributions, and dedication of many.

I wish to thank:

- The research teams. housing advocates, and organizations whose tireless work provided the foundation for much of the data and insight shared here.

- My colleagues and collaborators who reviewed drafts, offered critical feedback, and strengthened the vision behind this initiative.

- Finally, my family and community, whose unwavering belief in the transformative power of homeownership has been my deepest motivation.

To all of you — this work belongs as much to you as it does to me.

Why the Disparity in Homeownership?

Understanding the persistent gap in African American homeownership requires examining how multiple barriers work together to create compound disadvantages. Think of these barriers as interconnected obstacles rather than isolated problems. When we look at the most recent data from 2022-2025, we see that despite decades of policy intervention and civil rights progress, the fundamental disparities remain largely unchanged. The Black-white homeownership gap continues to hover around 27-28 percentage points, with African American homeownership at just 45.3-46.6% compared to 74.0-74.2% for non-Hispanic whites (National Association of Realtors, 2024)

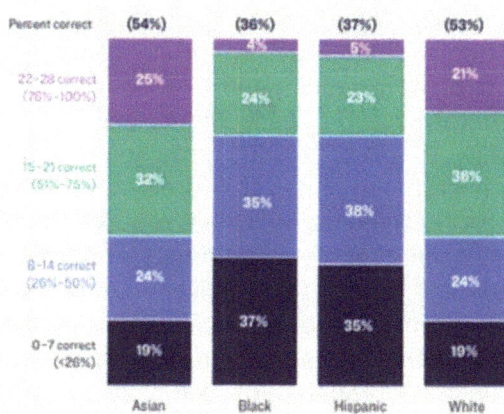

FIGURE 8. FINANCIAL LITERACY BY RACE AND ETHNICITY
Distribution of correct answers to *P-Fin Index* questions

Source: TIAA Institute-GFLEC Personal Finance Index (2024).

Figure 1. Financial Literacy by Race and Ethnicity. Source: TIAA Institute-GFLEC, Personal Finance Index (P-Fin Index), 2024.

1. This persistent gap tells us something crucial: homeownership disparities are not simply the result of individual choices or temporary market conditions. Instead, they reflect deep structural issues that compound over time, creating what economists call "cumulative disadvantage." When we examine each barrier individually, we begin to understand how they reinforce one another to create the overall disparity we observe today.

Poor Financial Literacy

Financial literacy represents the foundation upon which homeownership decisions rest. To understand why this matters so profoundly for African Americans, consider that purchasing a home involves navigating complex financial concepts including mortgage types, interest rates, down payment requirements, closing costs, property taxes, and insurance options. The ability to understand and compare these elements directly impacts whether someone can successfully become a homeowner and maintain that ownership over time.

The most comprehensive assessment of financial knowledge available today comes from the TIAA Institute-GFLEC Personal Finance Index, which measures understanding across eight functional areas essential for financial decision-making. The 2024 results reveal substantial and persistent knowledge gaps that help explain homeownership disparities. African Americans correctly answered only 36% of financial literacy questions compared to 53% for whites and 54% for Asian Americans (TIAA Institute-GFLEC, 2024). This 17 percentage point deficit has remained remarkably consistent across multiple survey cycles, suggesting that the gap represents more than temporary educational differences.

Breaking down these results by functional area reveals where the knowledge gaps are most severe. African Americans scored lowest in understanding risk management at 30% correct responses and insurance knowledge at also 30% correct. These areas are particularly relevant to homeownership because understanding risk helps potential buyers evaluate different mortgage products and insurance

Breaking down these results by functional area reveals where the knowledge gaps are most severe. African Americans scored lowest in understanding risk management at 30% correct responses and insurance knowledge at also 30% correct. These areas are particularly relevant to homeownership because understanding risk helps potential buyers evaluate different mortgage products and insurance

	Asian	Black	Hispanic	White
Borrowing	64% (1)	45% (1)	48% (1)	65% (1)
Saving	62% (2)	41% (3)	44% (2)	60% (2)
Consuming	54% (3)	42% (2)	43% (3)	52% (5)
Earning	49% (6)	37% (4)	37% (4)	53% (3)
Go-to info sources	53% (4)	35% (5)	34% (5)	53% (3)
Investing	53% (4)	32% (6)	33% (6)	50% (6)
Insuring	47% (7)	30% (7)	27% (8)	50% (6)
Comprehending risk	44% (8)	30% (7)	31% (7)	36% (8)

Source: TIAA Institute-GFLEC Personal Finance Index (2024).

Figure 2. Financial Literacy by Race and Ethnicity. Source: TIAA Institute-GFLEC, Personal Finance Index (P-Fin Index), 2024.

Perhaps most concerning is the distribution of overall performance levels. Only 5% of Black Americans demonstrated high financial performance by scoring 76-100% correct on the assessment, compared to 21% of whites and 25% of Asian Americans. At the other end of the spectrum, 37% of Black Americans scored in the very low performance category with less than 26% correct responses (TIAA Institute-GFLEC, 2024)[2]

This concentration of low scores suggests that a significant portion of the African American community lacks the basic financial knowledge necessary to navigate homeownership successfully.

The Federal Reserve's Survey of Household Economics and Decisionmaking provides additional context for understanding how financial knowledge translates into real-world capability. Only 68% of Black adults reported doing "at least okay" financially compared to 76% of white adults and 82% of Asian adults Federal Reserve, 2024). More specifically, the ability to cover a $400 emergency expense with cash remains significantly lower among Black households, indicating reduced financial resilience that directly impacts homebuying capacity and the ability to maintain homeownership once achieved. What makes these disparities particularly significant is that academic research published in 2024 confirms that educational attainment alone does not close racial financial literacy gaps (Annuity.org, 2024)

This finding suggests that systemic factors beyond individual knowledge acquisition contribute to persistent disparities in financial understanding and capability. The implication is that simply providing more financial education, while helpful, will not by itself eliminate the homeownership gap.

Legacy of Wage Disparity and Income Discrimination

Income and wealth form the economic foundation that makes homeownership possible or impossible. Understanding current disparities requires recognizing how historical discrimination has created cumulative disadvantages that persist across generations. When we examine today's wage gaps, we see the continuation of patterns that began with slavery, continued through Jim Crow, and persist despite civil rights legislation.

Current wage gap data demonstrates ongoing economic inequality that directly limits African Americans' ability to save for down payments, qualify for mortgages, and sustain homeownership costs. Black workers earn approximately 82% of white worker earnings, with median weekly earnings of $1,000 compared to $1,219 for white workers as of the first quarter of 2025 (Bureau of Labor Statistics, 2025)

To understand what this means in practical terms, consider that this weekly difference of $219 translates
to over $11,000 less annual income for full-time Black workers compared to their white counterparts.

The intersection of race and gender creates additional layers of disadvantage that compound these disparities. Black men earn 75.8% of white men's earnings, with weekly earnings of $1,017 compared to $1,342 for white men. Black women earn 89.2% of white women's earnings, bringing home $984 weekly compared to $1,103 for white women (Economic Policy Institute, 2024)

These differences may seem modest on a weekly basis, but they accumulate into substantial barriers over time. A Black man earning $12,200 less annually than his white counterpart will find it significantly more difficult to save the $50,000-80,000 typically needed for a down payment and closing costs on a median-priced home.

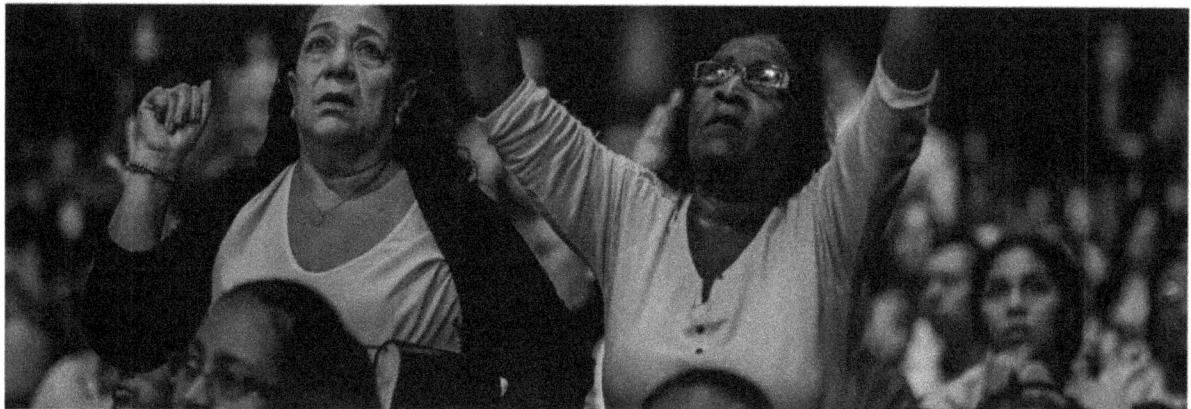

Wages for select demographic groups, 1979, 2019, and 2024 (2024$)

50th percentile wage	1979	2019	2024	Annualized percent change 1979–2019	Annualized percent change 2019–2024
All	$19.29	$23.52	$24.87	0.5%	1.1%
Male	$24.23	$25.48	$26.90	0.1%	1.1%
Female	$15.28	$21.54	$22.90	0.9%	1.2%
White	$19.97	$25.84	$27.28	0.6%	1.1%
Black	$16.66	$19.69	$21.40	0.4%	1.7%
Hispanic	$16.37	$19.07	$20.34	0.4%	1.3%
AAPI		$29.35	$31.35		1.3%
Race/ethnicity and gender					
White women	$15.49	$23.33	$24.78	1.0%	1.2%
White men	$25.43	$28.86	$29.89	0.3%	0.7%
Black women	$14.47	$19.05	$20.80	0.7%	1.8%
Black men	$19.20	$20.37	$22.13	0.1%	1.7%
Hispanic women	$13.52	$18.01	$19.53	0.7%	1.6%
Hispanic men	$18.85	$20.51	$21.76	0.2%	1.2%
Age					
16–24	$13.66	$14.66	$16.66	0.2%	2.6%
25+	$22.33	$25.46	$27.01	0.3%	1.2%
Education					
Less than a four-year degree	$18.25	$19.08	$20.13	0.1%	1.1%
Bachelor's degree or higher	$28.05	$36.09	$37.32	0.6%	0.7%

Note: AAPI refers to Asian American and Pacific Islander. Race/ethnicity categories are mutually exclusive (i.e., white non-Hispanic, Black non-Hispanic, AAPI non-Hispanic, and Hispanic any race).

Source: EPI analysis of the Current Population Survey Outgoing Rotation Group microdata, EPI Current Population Survey Extracts, Version 1.0.61 (2025a), https://microdata.epi.org.

Economic Policy Institute

The wealth gap reveals even starker disparities that help explain why income differences translate into homeownership gaps. The Federal Reserve's 2022 Survey of Consumer Finances shows Black families hold a median wealth of $44,900, representing only 15.7% of white family wealth of $285,000 (Federal Reserve, 2023)Think about what this means for homeownership: while both families might have similar incomes, the white family has over six times more accumulated wealth to draw upon for down payments, closing costs, moving expenses, and the inevitable repairs and improvements that

Figure 3. Wages for select demographic groups, 1979, 2019, and 2024 (2024$). Source: Economic Policy Institute, 2024.

Median Wealth

Mean Wealth

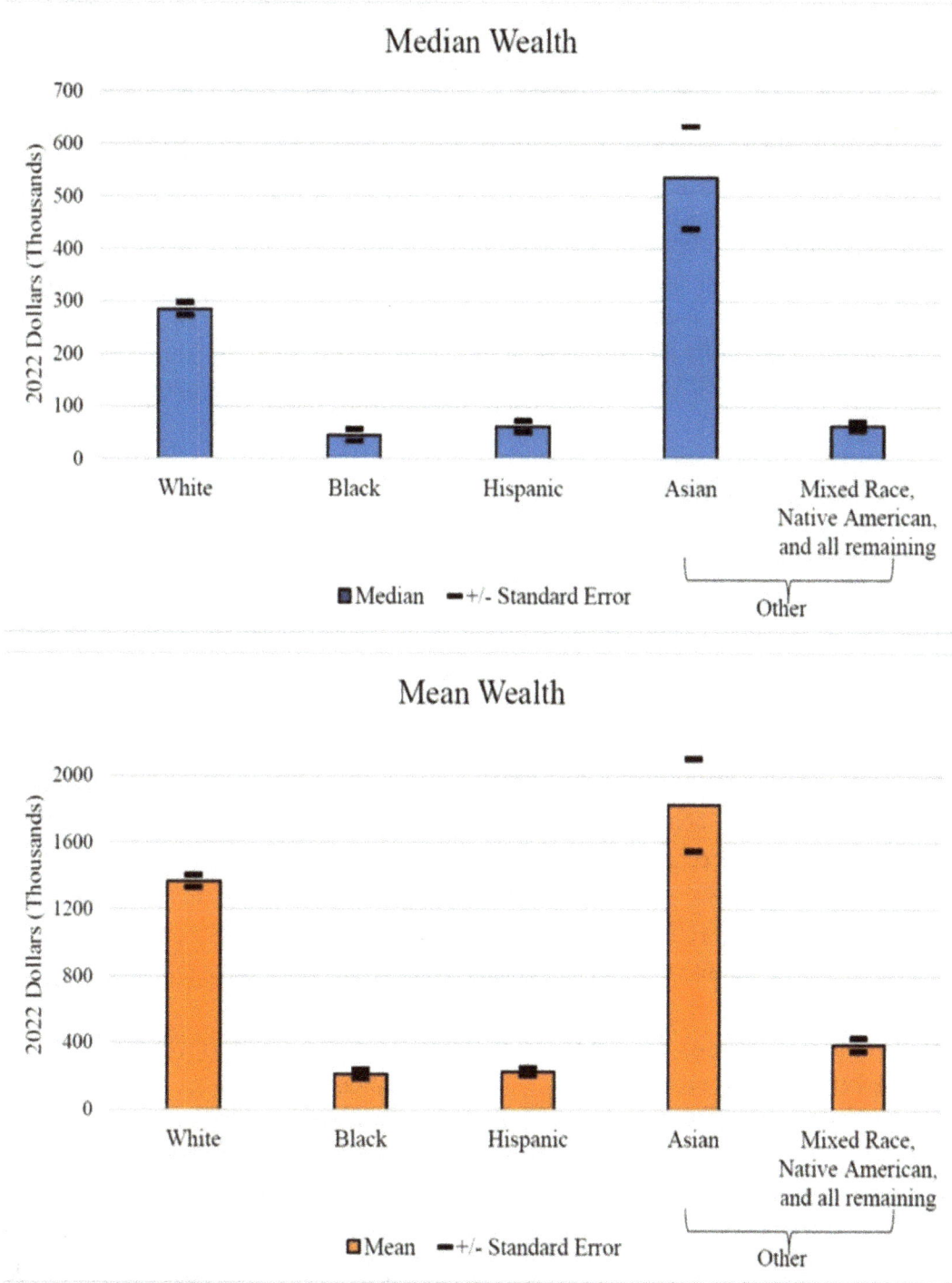

Figure 4. White and Asian Families Had the Most Wealth. Source: Board of Governors of the Federal Reserve System, 2023

What makes these wealth disparities particularly challenging is that despite significant percentage gains for Black families, absolute dollar gaps actually widened between 2019 and 2022. Black family wealth grew by 61% during this period, compared to 31% growth for white families. However, because Black families started from a much lower base, the absolute dollar gap increased by approximately $50,000 (Federal Reserve, 2023). This demonstrates how percentage gains can mask growing inequality in real terms and helps explain why homeownership gaps persist even during periods of economic growth.

In California, where The Power Is Now Media operates, these patterns intensify due to higher living costs and housing prices. Black women earn just 58 cents for every dollar earned by white men, while Latinas earn only 44 cents per dollar (Governing, 2024). Half of Latino, Black, and Native American workers in California earned $32,329 or less in 2021, while white men comprise 38% of top earners making $239,200 or more despite representing only 18% of the workforce (Fresnoland, 2024)7. These extreme disparities in California help explain why the state's Black homeownership rate remains among the lowest in the nation despite decades of policy intervention.

Home Loan Discrimination

Mortgage lending discrimination represents perhaps the most direct barrier to African American homeownership because it occurs at the precise moment when families attempt to transition from renting to owning. Understanding current lending disparities requires recognizing that discrimination has evolved from the overtly racist practices of redlining and racial covenants to more subtle but equally effective forms of bias in contemporary lending.

The most current Home Mortgage Disclosure Act data reveals continuing disparities in mortgage approval rates that cannot be explained by creditworthiness alone. Black mortgage applicants face denial rates of 16.4-19.0% compared to 5.8-11.27% for white applicants, representing denial rates that are 2.9 times higher for Black applicants (Consumer Financial Protection Bureau, 2024)8. To put this in perspective, if 100 equally qualified Black and white families applied for mortgages, approximately 17 Black families would be denied compared to only 6 white families.

Recent Federal Reserve research from Minneapolis provides particularly compelling evidence that these disparities cannot be explained by legitimate underwriting factors. Their 2024 study examined confidential HMDA data that included full credit scores and found that lender-reported denial reasons do not explain racial disparities (Federal Reserve Bank of Minneapolis, 2024)9. Even when controlling for credit history and financial qualifications, Black applicants remain 11.6% more likely to be denied for credit history reasons and 10.0% more likely to receive "Other" as a denial reason. The "Other" category is particularly concerning because it provides no transparency about the actual reasons for denial.

Race of applicant	Denial reason	Share of denied applications
Asian	Incomplete credit application	24.1%
	Unverifiable information	18.0%
	"Other"	16.8%
Black	Credit history	23.2%
	Insufficient collateral	19.4%
	Debt-to-income ratio	18.8%
Latino	Insufficient collateral	21.7%
	"Other"	17.9%
	Debt-to-income ratio	16.8%
White	Insufficient collateral	25.0%
	Incomplete credit application	21.5%
	"Other"	14.8%

Table 1: Top reasons for denials among denied applications differ by race and ethnicity of applicants.

Source: Confidential Home Mortgage Disclosure Act data (2018–2021) and authors' calculations

Understanding why these disparities persist requires examining the subtle ways bias can influence lending decisions. While overt discrimination based on race is illegal, research has identified several mechanisms through which disparate treatment occurs. These include differences in how loan officers interact with Black versus white applicants, variations in the effort exerted to help applicants improve their applications, disparities in the mortgage products offered, and differences in how discretionary underwriting guidelines are applied.

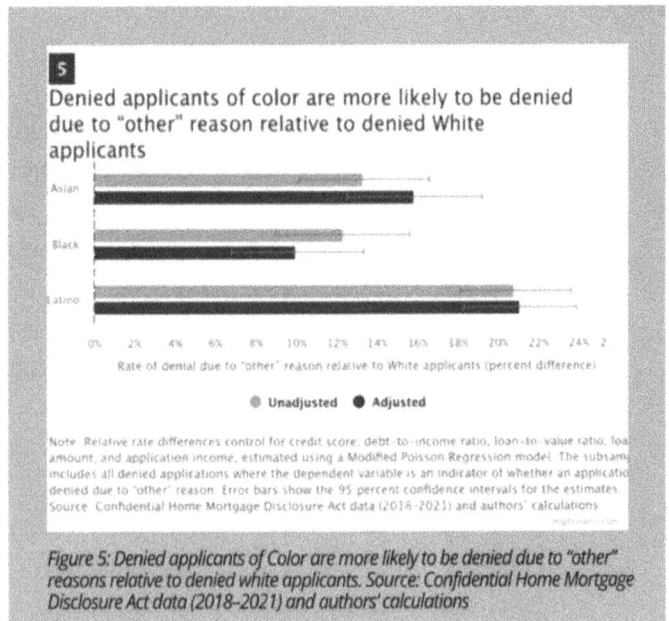

Figure 5: Denied applicants of Color are more likely to be denied due to "other" reasons relative to denied white applicants. Source: Confidential Home Mortgage Disclosure Act data (2018–2021) and authors' calculations

The Consumer Financial Protection Bureau's analysis reveals that Black applicants do have different average financial profiles, with median credit scores of 629 compared to approximately 729 for white applicants and higher average debt-to-income ratios of 40.0% versus 33.0% (Consumer Financial Protection Bureau, 2023)10. However, recent academic analysis of 1.4 million mortgage applications found that individual factors like income and debt-to-income ratios "barely account for racial disparities" in approval rates (PubMed Central, 2024)11. This finding suggests that while Black applicants may have different average profiles, the disparities in approval rates are far larger than these differences would predict.

California shows some variation in these patterns, with certain metropolitan areas performing better than national averages. San Francisco demonstrates only a 2.35 percentage point gap in denial rates between Black and white applicants, representing the smallest disparity nationally (National Association of Realtors, 2023)12. However, significant gaps persist in other California markets, and the state's high housing costs create additional barriers that disproportionately affect minority borrowers regardless of lending practices.

Limited Information and Outreach to African Americans

The final barrier involves how information about homeownership opportunities reaches African American communities and how effectively existing programs serve potential Black homebuyers. This barrier is particularly insidious because it operates through omission rather than commission, creating gaps in knowledge and access that may appear neutral but have disparate impacts.

Despite decades of homeownership promotion programs, evidence suggests limited effectiveness in reaching African American potential buyers. National Association of Realtors data shows that only 7% of recent homebuyers identify as Black or African American, significantly below the 13.6% Black share of the U.S. population (National Association of Realtors, 2024)1. This underrepresentation in the homebuying market suggests that either information about homeownership opportunities is not reaching Black communities effectively or that the information provided is not addressing the specific barriers they face.

Program awareness and utilization data reveals concerning gaps in how existing resources serve Black potential homebuyers. Research shows that 8% of Black homebuyers experienced race-based discrimination during the purchasing process, while 39% experienced discrimination in home appraisals (National Association of Realtors, 2023). These negative experiences likely discourage future participation and word-of-mouth referrals within Black communities, creating a cycle where discriminatory treatment reduces program effectiveness. Perhaps most troubling is evidence that traditional homebuyer education programs may not be effective for African American participants. HUD's comprehensive evaluation of first-time homebuyer education and counseling programs found that "the intervention had no detectable impact for African-American or Hispanic subgroups when compared to whites" (HUD User, 2024). This finding suggests that generic homebuying education programs may not address the specific barriers and challenges faced by minority homebuyers, including discrimination, limited wealth, and different risk profiles.

Real estate professionals, who serve as the primary information source for homebuyers, may lack knowledge about specialized programs and resources available to minority homebuyers. Current data shows that 86% of all buyers and 82% of Black buyers use real estate agents as their primary information source (National Association of Realtors, 2024)[1]. However, if these agents are not well-informed about down payment assistance programs, special lending products, or fair housing resources, they cannot effectively connect Black clients with the tools they need to overcome homeownership barriers.

California's targeted approach provides some evidence of what effective outreach might look like. The CalHFA Building Black Wealth Initiative served over 9,000 families using $165 million in down payment assistance, with aid concentrated in counties with significant African American populations (California Housing Finance Agency, 2021). However, state officials identify "education about the housing finance system and the inability to save for upfront costs" as the two biggest barriers Black Californians face (CalMatters, 2021)

This suggests that even targeted programs struggle to address the compound nature of homeownership barriers. Understanding how these four barriers work together helps explain why the African American homeownership gap has remained so persistent despite decades of policy intervention. Poor financial literacy makes it difficult to navigate mortgage options and understand true costs. Wage and wealth disparities limit the resources available for down payments and ongoing ownership costs. Lending discrimination creates additional hurdles at the point of purchase. Limited information and ineffective outreach mean that many potential Black homebuyers never learn about available resources or receive guidance that addresses their specific circumstances.

The interconnected nature of these barriers means that addressing any single factor is unlikely to eliminate homeownership disparities. Instead, effective solutions must recognize how financial literacy, economic inequality, lending discrimination, and information gaps reinforce each other to create cumulative disadvantages for African American families seeking homeownership.

African American Homeownership Initiative

The persistent disparities we examined in the previous chapters demand more than recognition—they require decisive action. The Power Is Now Media Inc.'s African American Homeownership Initiative represents our comprehensive response to the structural barriers that have prevented African American families from achieving homeownership at equitable rates. Drawing from the latest research and successful models from 2024-2025, our initiative recognizes that effective intervention must be as multifaceted as the problems we seek to address.

Recent developments in homeownership programming provide both inspiration and evidence for what works. The GroundBreak Coalition's 2024 investment of $1.5 million in capital to provide down payment assistance for 110 new Black homeowners demonstrates the power of targeted intervention (GroundBreak Coalition, 2024)

More ambitiously, their regional plan aims to unlock down payment assistance for 1,000 new homeowners over the next three years and 11,000 families over the decade. This scale of thinking—moving from individual transactions to systemic change—informs our approach.

Similarly, Twin Cities Habitat for Humanity's Advancing Black Homeownership Program has shown remarkable results using Special Purpose Credit Programs to serve Foundational Black Americans—those descended from enslaved Africans who have faced the steepest barriers to mortgage access (Twin Cities Habitat for Humanity, 2024)

Their program provides up to $50,000 for down payment assistance and utilizes flexible lending criteria that recognize how traditional credit requirements have systematically excluded Black households. California's Building Black Wealth initiative has served over 9,000 families using $165 million in down payment assistance, demonstrating the potential for state-level intervention (California Housing Finance Agency, 2024).

Our initiative builds upon these proven approaches while addressing the specific needs of communities we serve. We recognize that the 27-28 percentage point homeownership gap between African Americans and whites cannot be closed through traditional means alone. Instead, our strategy focuses on three foundational elements: Depower, Demystify, and Develop. Each element addresses different aspects of the systemic barriers we identified earlier, working together to create pathways to homeownership that were previously unavailable.

1. Our Strategy – Depower, Demystify and Develop

Our three-pronged strategy acknowledges that homeownership barriers operate at multiple levels simultaneously. Discrimination continues to limit access and increase costs. Complex financial systems remain opaque to many potential homebuyers. And without proper support, even successful homebuyers may struggle to maintain their ownership and build lasting wealth. Our strategy addresses each of these challenges systematically

The "Depower, Demystify, and Develop" framework emerged from studying both the failures of past approaches and the successes of current innovative programs. Traditional homeownership promotion often focused on individual preparation—improving credit scores, increasing savings, completing education courses—while leaving systemic barriers intact. More recent successful programs, like the Special Purpose Credit Programs now being implemented nationwide, recognize that individual preparation must be combined with systemic intervention. This integrated approach reflects lessons learned from recent fair housing enforcement data.

The National Fair Housing Alliance's 2024 Fair Housing Trends Report reveals that private nonprofit fair housing organizations processed 75.52% of housing discrimination complaints, representing a 5.68% increase from the previous year (National Fair Housing Alliance, 2024) 19 . Harassment complaints increased by 66.23%, and complaints based on color increased by 35.30%. These statistics underscore that discrimination remains a persistent force requiring active intervention, not passive hope that market forces will eventually create equity

	Race	Disability	Familial Status	Sex	National Origin	Color	Religion	Other	Total
NFHA Members	3,634	12,803	1,434	1,614	992	501	145	4,666	25,789
HUD	374	1,123	155	195	130	40	37	134	1,742
FHAPs	1,805	4,033	548	768	571	283	155	981	6,577
DOJ	7	9	2	11	0	0	0	13	42
Total	5,820	17,968	2,139	2,588	1,693	824	337	5,794	34,150
Percent of Total	17.04%	52.61%	6.26%	7.58%	4.96%	2.41%	0.99%	16.97%	

Figure 6: Complaint Data by Basis and Agency in 2023. Source: 2024 Fair Housing Trends Report

2. Depowering Discrimination

Discrimination represents perhaps the most fundamental barrier to African American homeownership because it operates at every stage of the housing process—from initial search through final approval and even post-purchase experiences. Our approach to depowering discrimination recognizes that we cannot eliminate prejudice from individual hearts, but we can reduce its power to limit housing opportunities through strategic intervention, education, and advocacy.

Recent developments in fair housing enforcement provide both challenges and opportunities for our work. HUD's announcement of $22.2 million in funding to combat housing discrimination through the Fair Housing Initiatives Program demonstrates continued federal commitment to enforcement (U.S. Department of Housing and Urban Development, 2024)

This funding supports fair housing education, outreach, testing, and enforcement activities across 75 organizations nationwide. However, the recent termination of 78 critical grants used to fight housing discrimination and the elimination of three-quarters of fair housing staff at HUD represents a significant setback (Center on Budget and Policy Priorities, 2025)

These policy changes make community-based initiatives like ours more crucial than ever. When federal enforcement weakens, local organizations must step forward to protect fair housing rights and create alternative pathways to homeownership. Our strategy includes several key components designed to reduce discrimination's impact on potential homebuyers.

Education and Collaboration form our first line of defense against discrimination. We partner with multicultural organizations that bring people together around shared homeownership goals rather than allowing discriminatory forces to divide communities. Recent research shows that when fair housing organizations use proactive testing and investigations rather than waiting for complaints, they uncover significantly more discrimination (HUD User, 2024) 22 . We apply this lesson by actively identifying discriminatory practices and educating both housing providers and potential homebuyers about fair housing rights

Legislative and Policy Advocacy represents our second strategic approach. We work with banking and real estate organizations that actively seek to hire diverse professionals and serve communities of color authentically. The Urban Institute's analysis of Fair Housing Act evolution demonstrates how advocacy has expanded protections over time, including recent court decisions extending protections based on sexual orientation and gender identity (Urban Institute, 2018) 23 . We build on this tradition by advocating for policies that address contemporary forms of discrimination, including algorithmic bias in lending and advertising platforms.

Professional Development and Industry Change constitute our third approach. We support efforts to increase diversity within real estate and mortgage lending professions, recognizing that representation matters for service quality. When potential homebuyers work with professionals who understand their communities and challenges, outcomes improve measurably. We provide training and resources to real estate professionals about fair housing requirements, available assistance programs, and cultural competency.

3. Demystify Homeownership

The complexity of homeownership in America has grown exponentially over recent decades, creating information barriers that disproportionately affect African American families. Traditional approaches to homebuyer education have shown limited effectiveness for minority populations, with HUD research finding that standard education programs had "no detectable impact for African-American or Hispanic subgroups when compared to whites" (HUD User, 2024) 13 . Our approach to demystifying homeownership therefore moves beyond generic education to provide targeted, accessible, culturally relevant information that addresses the specific challenges African American homebuyers face.

The evolution of homebuyer education provides important lessons for our approach. Fannie Mae's HomeView education course, which has served nearly 50,000 homebuyers since 2025, demonstrates the potential for well-designed online education (Fannie Mae, 2025) 24 . The course provides interactive, comprehensive guidance written in everyday language and designed for borrowers of all backgrounds. However, even excellent generic programs may not address the specific discrimination-related challenges African American homebuyers encounter.

Accessible Information Delivery represents our core strategy for demystification. As a media company, we are uniquely positioned to provide information in formats that work for different learning styles and schedules. Our online seminars, video content, and interactive resources allow potential homebuyers to access information anytime, anywhere, and on-demand. We translate complex financial concepts into practical guidance that directly relates to the experiences of African American families

Recent technological developments enhance our ability to provide accessible education. Framework Homeowner Education now offers courses in both English and Spanish with audio options, recognizing that language accessibility improves outcomes (Framework Homeownership, 2025) 25 . We apply similar principles by providing content in multiple formats and languages as needed by our communities.

Addressing Specific Barriers sets our educational approach apart from generic programs. We explicitly address how discrimination affects the homebuying process, what legal protections exist, and how to respond to unfair treatment. Our educational content includes information about Special Purpose Credit Programs, down payment assistance specifically available to African American families, and strategies for working with real estate professionals who may lack cultural competency

Ongoing Support and Mentorship extend beyond traditional education completion. We recognize that homebuying involves ongoing decisions and challenges that arise after initial education. Our approach includes mentorship relationships with successful African American homeowners, ongoing financial coaching, and support networks that help families navigate challenges that arise during and after the homebuying process

4. Develop Homeowners

Successful homeownership requires more than completing a purchase transaction—it demands ongoing financial management, property maintenance, and wealth-building strategies that many first-time buyers may not have learned from family experience. Our development approach recognizes that African American families are more likely to be first-generation homeowners without family knowledge to draw upon, making structured support essential for long-term success.

Recent research on homeownership sustainability provides important guidance for our development strategy. The U.S. Treasury's Homeowner Assistance Fund has assisted over 549,000 homeowners through June 2024, helping prevent foreclosures and displacement (U.S. Department of the Treasury, 2025) 26 . The program's success in reaching economically vulnerable and traditionally underserved homeowners, including 39% who identified as Black, demonstrates both the need for ongoing support and the effectiveness of targeted assistance.

Strategic Partnerships with Community Organizations form the foundation of our development approach. We work with housing finance agencies, churches, nonprofit organizations, and community groups that already serve African American communities. Rather than duplicating existing services, we become their strategic partner to provide and disseminate information and create opportunities for their constituents to learn about homeownership, obtain loan approval, identify real estate professionals, and find homes to purchase.

Recent examples demonstrate the power of this partnership approach. Twin Cities Habitat's Advancing Black Homeownership Program includes partnerships with the GroundBreak Coalition to provide systematic down payment assistance through a combination of grants and interest-free loans (GroundBreak Coalition, 2024) 17 . These no-interest loans require no monthly payments and are repaid only when the property is sold or refinanced, removing traditional debt burdens that might prevent homeownership sustainability.

Financial Coaching and Wealth Building extend beyond initial homebuying education to help families maximize the wealth-building potential of homeownership. We provide ongoing coaching on mortgage management, property maintenance budgeting, refinancing decisions, and strategies for paying off mortgages early. Our coaching recognizes that homeownership represents the foundation for generational wealth building, not just a housing solution.

Professional Network Development connects new homeowners with trusted service providers who understand their communities and economic circumstances. We maintain networks of contractors, financial advisors, insurance agents, and other professionals who have demonstrated commitment to serving African American homeowners fairly and competently. This network helps homeowners avoid predatory services that target minority communities.

5. Our Second Strategy – To Be a Homeownership Resource

While our initial focus targets the African American community where we have established relationships and expertise, our broader vision encompasses becoming a comprehensive homeownership resource for all communities facing barriers to homeownership. This expansion strategy recognizes that many of the systemic issues affecting African American homeownership also impact other marginalized communities, while acknowledging that each community faces unique challenges requiring tailored approaches.

The National Association of Real Estate Brokers' Two Million New Black Homeowners Program (2MN5) provides a model for how focused community-specific initiatives can contribute to broader housing equity (National Association of Real Estate Brokers, 2019) 27 . Their program combines advocacy for Black homeownership, access to credit, neighborhood development projects, and business development training. By succeeding in serving the African American community first, they build capacity and expertise that can inform work with other communities.

Multicultural Initiative Development represents our planned expansion to serve Asian American, Latino American, LGBTQ+, and low-to-moderate-income communities through specialized initiatives. Each initiative will maintain our three-pronged approach of Depower, Demystify, and Develop while addressing the specific discrimination patterns, information gaps, and development needs of different communities.

Recent fair housing data demonstrates why community-specific approaches remain necessary. While disability-based discrimination accounts for 52.61% of fair housing complaints, racial discrimination continues to represent significant portions of complaints, with harassment complaints increasing dramatically (National Fair Housing Alliance, 2024) 19 . Different communities face different patterns of discrimination requiring tailored intervention strategies.

Resource Coordination and Information Sharing will connect our community-specific initiatives to share effective strategies and avoid duplicating efforts. We envision our media platform serving as a central hub where real estate professionals and minority consumers nationwide can access information about programs, services, and opportunities relevant to their communities.

Professional Development and Industry Change extends our discrimination-fighting work to benefit all communities. As we train real estate professionals about fair housing requirements and cultural competency for serving African American clients, we simultaneously build their capacity to serve other marginalized communities more effectively

Professional Development and Industry Change extends our discrimination-fighting work to benefit all communities. As we train real estate professionals about fair housing requirements and cultural competency for serving African American clients, we simultaneously build their capacity to serve other marginalized communities more effectively.

The foundation we build through focused work in the African American community creates a platform for expanding impact across all communities that face homeownership barriers. Our experience addressing the specific challenges of racial discrimination, financial literacy gaps, and wealth disparities provides expertise that can inform work with other communities while respecting their unique needs and circumstances.

Our African American Homeownership Initiative represents more than a program—it constitutes a comprehensive approach to addressing the structural barriers that have maintained homeownership disparities for generations. By combining discrimination-fighting strategies, accessible education, ongoing development support, and community partnerships, we create pathways to homeownership that traditional approaches have failed to provide. The success of this initiative will demonstrate the potential for targeted, community-based intervention to achieve the systemic change necessary for housing equity.

The Plight of African American Homeownership

The story of African American homeownership in America represents one of the most profound illustrations of how systemic discrimination can persist across generations, adapting to changing times while maintaining its fundamental character. Understanding the current plight requires recognizing that today's homeownership disparities are not accidents of the market or reflections of individual choices, but rather the predictable outcomes of centuries of intentional exclusion followed by decades of inadequate remedy.

Recent data reveals the stark persistence of these disparities. As of 2024, the Black homeownership rate stands at 46.4%, compared to 74.4% for white households—a gap of 28 percentage points that has remained virtually unchanged for decades (Bankrate, 2025) 28 . More troubling still, this gap is actually wider today than it was when the Fair Housing Act of 1968 was signed into law. In 2019, the homeownership gap between white and Black populations was larger than the gap in the 1960s, before the Civil Rights Movement had achieved its landmark legislative victories (Ballard Brief, 2025)

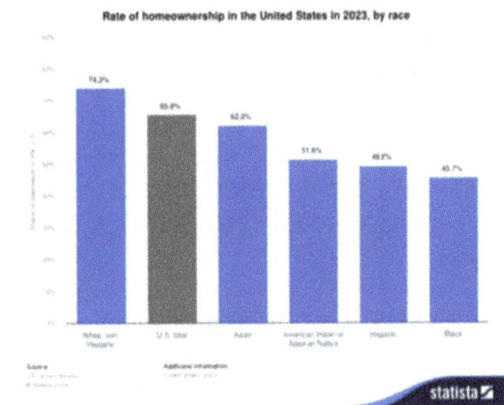

Figure 7: Rate of homeownership in the United States in 2023, by race. Source: Statista, 2023.

The National Association of Realtors' 2024 analysis reveals that Black Americans continue to face the steepest barriers to homeownership of any racial group. While Asian Americans achieved record homeownership rates of 63% and Hispanic Americans reached 51.1%—also a record high— Black homeownership saw only modest gains to 44.1% in 2022, remaining substantially below all other major ethnic groups (National Association of Realtors, 2024) 30 . These disparities persist across income levels, suggesting that the barriers to Black homeownership extend far beyond simple economic factors

This persistence demands explanation because it contradicts the narrative of steady progress that many Americans prefer to believe about racial equity. The uncomfortable truth is that while overt discrimination became illegal, the systems that created advantage for white families and disadvantage for Black families largely remained intact. The mechanisms evolved, becoming more subtle but no less effective in maintaining racial hierarchies in homeownership and wealth accumulation

The National Association of Realtors' 2024 analysis reveals that Black Americans continue to face the steepest barriers to homeownership of any racial group. While Asian Americans achieved record homeownership rates of 63% and Hispanic Americans reached 51.1%—also a record high— Black homeownership saw only modest gains to 44.1% in 2022, remaining substantially below all other major ethnic groups (National Association of Realtors, 2024) 30 . These disparities persist across income levels, suggesting that the barriers to Black homeownership extend far beyond simple economic factors

Even more revealing is the geographic variation in these disparities. Black homeownership rates range from as low as 19% in Wyoming and North Dakota to 57% in Mississippi (CNN Business, 2024) 31 . This variation reflects how local conditions—from employment opportunities to discriminatory practices to the presence of historically Black institutions—can either exacerbate or partially mitigate national patterns of exclusion.

The urgency of addressing this plight has intensified because of recent market conditions. The Urban Institute warns that high interest rates threaten to further widen racial homeownership gaps, potentially erasing modest gains made during the pandemic when low rates briefly expanded access (Urban Institute, 2025) 32 . Between 2019 and 2022, only 43% of Black renters could afford a median-priced home nationwide, compared to 35% for white renters—a disparity that has grown as housing costs have outpaced income growth for all Americans but hit minority communities hardest

Understanding this plight requires recognizing how multiple disadvantages compound over time. Lower homeownership rates mean less wealth accumulation, which means fewer resources for down payments, which perpetuates lower homeownership rates. The Federal Reserve's data shows that Black families hold median wealth of only $44,900 compared to $285,000 for white families—a ratio that has changed little despite recent economic growth (U.S. Department of the Treasury, 2022) 33 . When homeownership represents the primary vehicle for wealth building for most American families, this disparity becomes self-perpetuating across generations.

The plight extends beyond individual families to entire communities. As HUD researchers note, residential segregation remains "the bedrock of all inequality in America," with its effects manifesting in unequal access to quality schools, employment opportunities, healthcare, and other community resources (HUD User, 2021) 34 . Communities with low homeownership rates struggle to attract and retain businesses, maintain property values, and provide stable environments for children's development

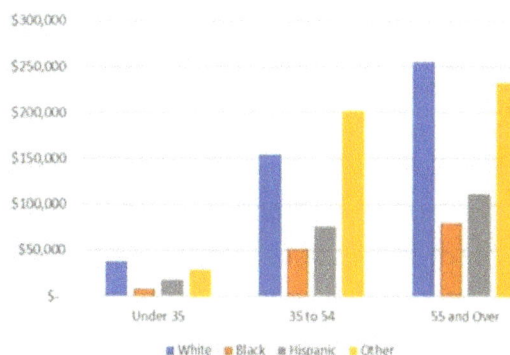

Figure 8: Racial Differences in Housing Equity Wealth Over the Lifecycle, 2019. Source: U.S. Department of the Treasury, 2022.

Recent research has also highlighted how discrimination has evolved with technology. The National Fair Housing Alliance's Tech Equity Initiative identifies significant risks in algorithmic systems used for risk assessment and automated underwriting, which can perpetuate bias in more sophisticated but equally harmful ways (HUD User, 2021) 24 . When 70% of new households between 2021 and 2025 are expected to be minority-headed, addressing these technological forms of discrimination becomes essential for any meaningful progress.

The COVID-19 pandemic briefly offered hope for progress. Black homeownership gained 2 percentage points between 2019 and 2021 as historically low interest rates expanded access. However, these gains proved fragile. As interest rates rose dramatically in 2022 and 2023, Black mortgage originations fell by more than 16%, while Black mortgage denial rates increased by 2.6 percentage points—higher than the increases experienced by other racial groups (Urban Wire, 2023)

This recent reversal illustrates how quickly progress can be lost when underlying structural issues remain unaddressed. It also demonstrates that market conditions alone—even favorable ones like historically low interest rates—cannot overcome the compound disadvantages that African American families face in pursuing homeownership.

The plight of African American homeownership thus represents both historical legacy and contemporary reality. It reflects centuries of intentional exclusion that created massive advantages for white families while denying similar opportunities to Black families. But it also reflects ongoing discrimination, inadequate policy responses, and market conditions that continue to disproportionately harm minority communities. Understanding this plight in its full complexity is essential for developing effective responses that can finally begin to close gaps that have persisted for far too long.

The State of Black Homeownership

Examining the current state of Black homeownership requires moving beyond broad national statistics to understand how geographic, demographic, and economic factors create vastly different experiences for African American families seeking to build wealth through homeownership. The most recent comprehensive data reveals a complex landscape where modest gains in some areas are offset by persistent barriers that continue to limit opportunities for the majority of Black families

Current federal data shows that as of the fourth quarter of 2023, Black homeownership stands at 45.9%, representing a 2.7 percentage point increase from 43.2% a decade earlier (Eye on Housing, 2024) 35 While this represents the largest percentage increase among racial groups during this period, it falls far short of closing the racial homeownership gap. Non-Hispanic white homeownership increased only marginally during the same period, from 73.4% to 73.8%, but starting from such a high baseline meant that the absolute gap between Black and white homeownership actually widened despite Black families making larger percentage gains.

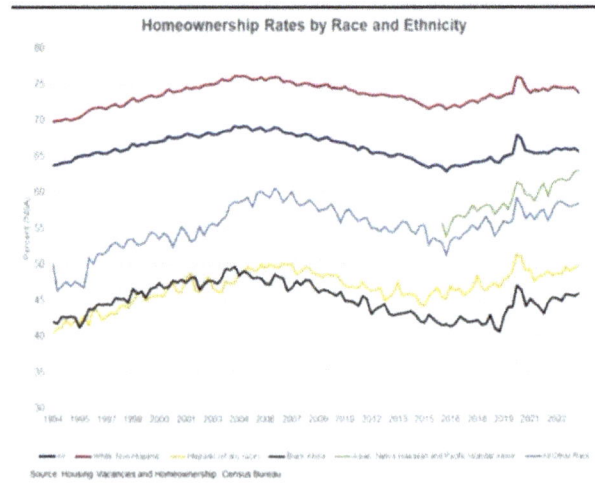

Figure 9: Homeownership Rates by Race and Ethnicity . Source: National Association of Home Builders Eye on Housing, 2024.

The geographic distribution of Black homeownership reveals striking disparities that reflect regional economic conditions, historical migration patterns, and varying levels of discrimination. Southern states generally show higher Black homeownership rates, with Mississippi leading at 57%, followed by South Carolina and Delaware at 55% each (National Association of Realtors, 2024) 30 . These higher rates often reflect lower housing costs, the presence of historically Black colleges and universities, and stronger extended family networks that can provide financial support for homebuying

Conversely, northern and western metropolitan areas frequently show the largest homeownership gaps between Black and white families. Minneapolis demonstrates the most extreme disparity, with a 50 percentage point gap between Black and white homeownership rates. Albany, New York follows with a 49 percentage point gap (Urban Institute, 2018) 36 . These northern cities often have smaller but more isolated Black populations, higher housing costs relative to local Black incomes, and less intergenerational wealth accumulation due to more recent migration patterns from the South.

California presents a particularly challenging environment for Black homeownership, reflecting both the state's extreme housing costs and its history of discriminatory practices. The UC Berkeley Othering & Belonging Institute's analysis shows that Black homeownership in California declined from 40% to 35% between 1980 and 2020—the only racial group to experience a decrease during this period (Othering & Belonging Institute, 2024) 37 . This decline occurred while other racial groups achieved historic peaks in their homeownership rates, making the relative position of Black Californians even worse.

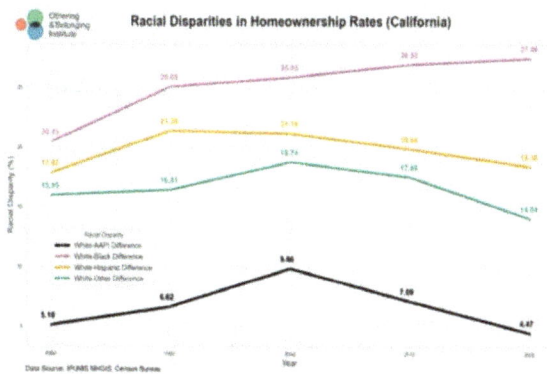

Figure 10: Racial Disparities in Homeownership rates (California). Source: IPUMS NHGIS: Census Bureau, 2025.

The age demographics of Black homeowners reveal concerning trends about future homeownership prospects. Younger Black families face particularly steep barriers, with only 33% of Black millennials owning homes compared to 65% of white millennials—the largest generational gap on record (Redfin, 2024) 18 . This pattern suggests that unless significant interventions occur, future Black homeownership rates may actually decline as older homeowners age out of the market without being replaced by younger Black homebuyers.

Recent market conditions have created additional challenges for prospective Black homeowners. The National Association of Realtors reports that 62% of Black homebuyers in 2024 were first-time purchasers, maintaining the same high percentage as 2023 despite overall declines in first-time buying (HousingWire, 2025)

This concentration among first-time buyers reflects both the limited intergenerational wealth transfer within Black families and the particular challenges first-time buyers face in competitive housing markets.

Affordability represents the most immediate barrier to expanding Black homeownership. Current data shows that only 17.6% of listings are considered affordable for the average Black household, compared to significantly higher percentages for other racial groups (HousingWire, 2025) 30 . This affordability crisis reflects both lower median incomes—$56,490 for Black households compared to $84,630 for white households according to 2024 Census data—and systematically higher housing costs in many areas where Black families live (LendingTree, 2025

The intersection of homeownership and wealth accumulation continues to perpetuate racial disparities across generations. Census Bureau analysis shows that white households hold ten times more wealth than Black households, with much of this disparity attributable to differences in homeownership and home equity accumulation (U.S. Census Bureau, 2024) 40 . Black households are more likely to have student loan debt (25.8% versus 17.2% for white households) and medical debt (22.5% versus 13.4%), reducing their capacity to save for down payments and maintain homeownership once achieved.

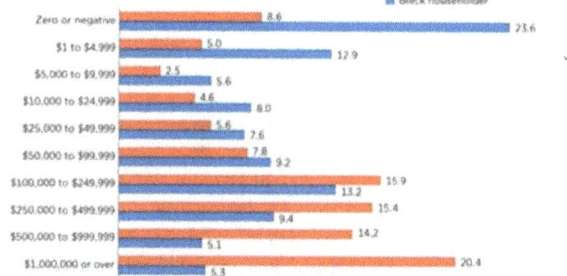

Figure 11: Distribution of Household Net Worth by Amount of Net Worth and Race of Householder. Source: U.S. Census Bureau Survey of Income and Program Participation (SIPP), 2024.

Recent fair housing enforcement data reveals that discrimination continues to limit Black homeownership opportunities. The 2024 Fair Housing Trends Report documents that complaints based on color increased by 35.30%, while harassment complaints increased by 66.23% (National Fair Housing Alliance, 2024) 19 . These statistics likely underrepresent the true extent of discrimination, as many instances go unreported or are difficult to prove using traditional investigation methods.

The lending landscape shows persistent disparities in both access and terms. Black mortgage applicants face denial rates of approximately 20% compared to 11% for white applicants, with recent Federal Reserve research finding that these disparities cannot be explained by legitimate underwriting factors (Federal Reserve Bank of Minneapolis, 2024) 9 . Even when Black families successfully obtain mortgages, they often receive less favorable terms, with 20% of Black borrowers receiving interest rates above 6% compared to 18% of white borrowers.

Technology represents both an opportunity and a threat for expanding Black homeownership. While online education platforms and digital mortgage applications can improve access, algorithmic bias in credit scoring and automated underwriting systems may perpetuate discrimination in more sophisticated forms. The National Fair Housing Alliance's Tech Equity Initiative has identified significant risks in these systems that require active intervention to prevent digital redlining from replacing traditional forms of discrimination.

State and local initiatives provide some hope for progress. California's Building Black Wealth initiative has served over 9,000 families with $165 million in down payment assistance, demonstrating the potential impact of targeted interventions (California Housing Finance Agency, 2024) 18 . However, the scale of these programs remains insufficient to address the magnitude of the homeownership gap, and funding limitations mean many eligible families cannot access available assistance

The current state of Black homeownership thus presents a paradox: modest statistical gains that mask persistent structural barriers and growing absolute disparities. While Black families have increased their homeownership rates more rapidly than other groups in percentage terms, they remain far behind in absolute terms and face intensifying affordability challenges that threaten to reverse recent progress.

1. Wealth Inequalities

The relationship between wealth and homeownership creates a self-reinforcing cycle that helps explain why racial homeownership gaps have proven so resistant to change over time. Understanding current wealth inequalities provides essential context for comprehending both the barriers to Black homeownership and the potential impact of successful policy interventions.

The most recent Federal Reserve Survey of Consumer Finances reveals the staggering extent of racial wealth disparities. In 2022, the median wealth of white households reached $285,000, while Black households held median wealth of just $44,900—a ratio of approximately 6.3 to 1 (Federal Reserve, 2023) 3 . This disparity has persisted despite Black families experiencing 61% wealth growth between 2019 and 2022, compared to 31% growth for white families. While the percentage gains for Black families were higher, the absolute dollar gap actually widened by approximately $50,000 during this period, demonstrating how percentage improvements can mask growing inequality in real terms.

The composition of wealth reveals why homeownership represents such a crucial factor in addressing racial inequality. For Black homeowners, home equity comprises 67% of their median net worth, compared to 58% for white homeowners despite white families having substantially higher homeownership rates and median home values (Survey of Income and Program Participation, 2022).

This concentration means that Black families' financial security depends heavily on homeownership, making exclusion from housing markets particularly devastating for wealth accumulation.

Recent Census Bureau analysis provides additional perspective on how wealth disparities manifest across different asset categories. White households are 1.1 times more likely to have basic checking and savings accounts, but conditional on ownership, hold median account values 5.4 times larger than Black households—$13,500 compared to $2,500 (U.S. Census Bureau, 2024) 40 . For investment assets, the disparities become even more pronounced, with white households holding median investment values multiple times higher than Black households across nearly every category.

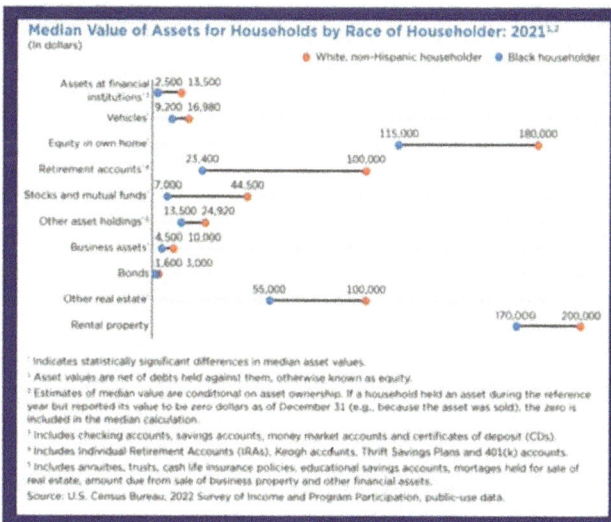

Median Value of Assets for Households by Race of Householder: 2021[1,2]
(In dollars)

● White, non-Hispanic householder ● Black householder

Assets at financial institutions[3]	2,500 13,500
Vehicles	9,200 16,980
Equity in own home	115,000 180,000
Retirement accounts[4]	23,400 100,000
Stocks and mutual funds[4]	7,000 44,500
Other asset holdings[5]	13,500 24,920
Business assets[5]	4,500 10,000
Bonds	1,600 3,000
Other real estate	55,000 100,000
Rental property	170,000 200,000

[1] Indicates statistically significant differences in median asset values.
[1] Asset values are net of debts held against them, otherwise known as equity.
[2] Estimates of median value are conditional on asset ownership. If a household held an asset during the reference year but reported its value to be zero dollars as of December 31 (e.g., because the asset was sold), the zero is included in the median calculation.
[3] Includes checking accounts, savings accounts, money market accounts and certificates of deposit (CDs).
[4] Includes Individual Retirement Accounts (IRAs), Keogh accounts, Thrift Savings Plans and 401(k) accounts.
[5] Includes annuities, trusts, cash life insurance policies, educational savings accounts, mortgages held for sale of real estate, amount due from sale of business property and other financial assets.
Source: U.S. Census Bureau, 2022 Survey of Income and Program Participation, public-use data.

Figure 12: Median Value of Assets for Households by Race of Householder. Source: U.S. Census Bureau Survey of Income and Program Participation (SIPP), 2024.

The debt profile of Black families further constrains their ability to build wealth through homeownership. Black households are more likely than white households to carry unsecured debt (61.3% versus 53.4%), particularly student loan debt (25.8% versus 17.2%) and medical debt (22.5% versus 13.4%). This debt burden reduces families' capacity to save for down payments and may affect their debt-to-income ratios in ways that limit mortgage qualification or result in less favorable loan terms.

Intergenerational wealth transfer represents another crucial factor in perpetuating homeownership disparities. Research consistently shows that family financial support serves as a major driver of homeownership, particularly for first-time buyers who may receive assistance with down payments, closing costs, or ongoing mortgage support during financial difficulties. The Urban Institute estimates that white families are significantly more likely to receive such support and receive larger amounts when assistance is provided.

Income disparities, while smaller than wealth disparities, continue to limit Black families' capacity to build wealth through homeownership. The most recent Bureau of Labor Statistics data shows Black workers earning approximately 82% of white worker earnings, with median weekly earnings of $1,000 compared to $1,219 for white workers (Economic Policy Institute, 2024) 5 . These income gaps translate directly into reduced capacity to save for down payments and maintain homeownership once achieved.

The geographic concentration of wealth also affects homeownership opportunities. Black families are more likely to live in areas with limited access to mainstream financial services, higher crime rates, and lower property values—all factors that can limit wealth accumulation through homeownership even when families successfully purchase homes. The Brookings Institution's analysis shows that homes in predominantly Black neighborhoods are valued at $48,000 less than comparable homes in predominantly white neighborhoods, representing a cumulative loss in equity of approximately $156 billion (National League of Cities, 2024)

Credit access represents another dimension of wealth inequality that directly affects homeownership opportunities. Black families are more likely to live in "credit deserts"—areas with limited access to mainstream credit products—which can result in lower credit scores that limit mortgage qualification. Even when Black families have good credit, they may lack the credit history depth that helps secure the most favorable mortgage terms, as their families may have less experience with credit products due to historical exclusion from mainstream financial services.

Recent economic shocks have highlighted how wealth disparities affect families' ability to maintain homeownership during difficult periods. The COVID-19 pandemic disproportionately affected Black workers through job losses and reduced hours, while Black families had fewer financial reserves to weather these disruptions. The federal Homeowner Assistance Fund ultimately served 39% Black homeowners among its beneficiaries, reflecting both their higher risk of housing instability and their lower baseline wealth that made recovery more difficult.

Business ownership represents another avenue for wealth building that shows significant racial disparities. Recent Federal Reserve data indicates that Black business ownership grew markedly during the 2019-2022 period, but from a much lower baseline than white business ownership. Success in business ownership can provide resources for homeownership, but the historical exclusion of Black entrepreneurs from capital markets and business networks has limited this pathway for wealth accumulation.

The stock market represents an increasingly important component of wealth building for American families, with significant implications for homeownership capacity. Recent data shows that all racial groups increased their stock market participation, but Black families saw the largest percentage increase from a lower baseline. However, Black families remain significantly less likely to own stocks and hold smaller portfolios when they do participate, limiting their ability to build wealth through market appreciation.

Retirement savings represent another crucial component of wealth that can affect homeownership in multiple ways. Families with substantial retirement savings may have more flexibility in timing home purchases, accessing funds for down payments through retirement account loans, or maintaining homeownership during periods of reduced income. Black families consistently show lower retirement account balances and are less likely to have employer-sponsored retirement benefits, further limiting their financial flexibility around homeownership decisions

Educational debt specifically represents a growing barrier to homeownership that disproportionately affects Black families. Black college graduates carry average student loan debt of $23,420 compared to $16,046 for white graduates, and they are more likely to attend schools requiring unsubsidized loans that accrue interest during enrollment. This debt burden directly competes with saving for homeownership and may affect debt-to-income ratios used in mortgage underwriting.

2. Black Immigrants

The experience of Black immigrants in the American housing market provides important insights into how both racial discrimination and immigrant status affect homeownership opportunities. Recent research reveals that Black immigrants face a unique combination of challenges that result in homeownership rates substantially below both the general population and native-born Black Americans, while also highlighting how factors beyond race influence housing outcomes.

According to the Joint Center for Housing Studies at Harvard University, approximately 12.4% of Black households nationwide are led by immigrants, representing slightly less than one in eight Black households. However, this proportion varies dramatically by state, with states having the highest percentages of immigrant-led Black households often having lower numbers of native-born Black households. This geographic distribution reflects broader immigration patterns and economic opportunities that attract Black immigrants to specific regions.

Foreign-born Black households demonstrate significantly lower homeownership rates than their U.S.-born counterparts. According to Pew Research Center analysis, only 40% of Black immigrants are homeowners compared to 64% of Americans overall (Urban Institute, 2018) 36 . When compared specifically with other immigrant groups, foreign-born Black people are less likely to own homes than immigrants generally, suggesting that racial discrimination compounds the typical barriers that immigrants face in accessing homeownership.

Economic factors explain some but not all of these disparities. The median household income for Black immigrants was $57,200 in recent Pew research, which exceeds the median income for Black Americans overall but falls below the $63,000 median for all U.S. immigrants. This income positioning reflects the complex relationship between race, immigration status, and economic opportunity in America, where Black immigrants may benefit from selective migration that brings higher-skilled workers to the United States while still facing racial discrimination in housing and employment markets.

Regional differences in Black immigrant experiences reflect varying economic opportunities and community support systems. Caribbean-born households show the highest median income within Black immigrant communities at $58,200, followed by African-born households at $54,000, and Central American or Mexican-born Black households at $50,000. These income differences correlate with homeownership rates and reflect different educational backgrounds, professional networks, and community resources available to immigrants from different regions.

The poverty rates among Black immigrant communities provide additional context for understanding homeownership barriers. Prior to the COVID-19 pandemic, 14% of Black immigrants lived below the poverty threshold, which was higher than the 11% rate for all Black Americans but lower than the 19% rate for native-born Black Americans. This positioning suggests that while selective migration may provide some economic advantages, Black immigrants still face significant financial challenges that limit their homeownership opportunities.

Length of residence in the United States significantly affects Black immigrant homeownership rates, as with other immigrant groups. Recent Pew Research analysis shows that typical immigrants in 2008 had spent more years in the U.S. and were more likely to be U.S. citizens than typical immigrants in 1995, factors strongly associated with higher homeownership rates. This trend helped mitigate recent housing market troubles among immigrants generally, but Black immigrants may not have benefited equally due to persistent racial discrimination in housing markets.

Credit access represents a particular challenge for Black immigrants, who may lack the credit history necessary for favorable mortgage terms while also facing the racial discrimination that affects all Black homebuyers. Recent immigrants may have excellent financial records in their countries of origin but find these credentials difficult to translate into American credit scores. This challenge is compounded for Black immigrants who may face discrimination from lenders even when they successfully establish U.S. credit histories.

Cultural factors also influence Black immigrant homeownership patterns, as different immigrant communities bring varying attitudes toward homeownership, extended family living arrangements, and wealth building strategies. Some Black immigrant communities prioritize business ownership or supporting family members in countries of origin over homeownership, while others view homeownership as essential for establishing roots in American communities.

The concentration of Black immigrants in high-cost metropolitan areas creates additional barriers to homeownership. Cities like New York, Washington D.C., and Los Angeles attract significant Black immigrant populations due to economic opportunities and established communities, but these same areas often have housing costs that make homeownership difficult even for middle-income families.

The Urban Institute's mapping analysis shows that expensive metropolitan areas like Los Angeles have Black homeownership rates of only 33.5%, reflecting how high housing costs can overwhelm other factors.

Language barriers may affect some Black immigrant communities' access to homeownership information and services, though many Black immigrants come from English-speaking countries or have strong English skills. However, the complexity of American mortgage and real estate systems may still create information barriers that require targeted outreach and education to overcome.

Discrimination against Black immigrants may take multiple forms, including both racial discrimination that affects all Black Americans and xenophobic discrimination that affects immigrants generally. Recent fair housing testing has identified instances where immigrants face discrimination based on accent, name, or perceived foreign status, in addition to racial discrimination. For Black immigrants, these forms of discrimination may combine to create particularly severe barriers to housing access.

Recent policy changes affecting immigration status can impact Black immigrant homeownership in multiple ways. Uncertainties about legal status may make families reluctant to make long-term commitments like homeownership, while changes in immigration policy can affect employment authorization and income stability. The intersection of housing policy and immigration policy creates complex challenges that require coordinated responses.

Community organizations serving Black immigrant populations often identify homeownership as a priority but may lack the specialized knowledge necessary to navigate American real estate and mortgage systems effectively. Successful programs often combine culturally competent outreach with technical expertise about available mortgage products, down payment assistance programs, and fair housing protections.

The success of Black immigrants in achieving homeownership despite facing multiple barriers provides important lessons for expanding homeownership opportunities more broadly. Understanding which factors help Black immigrant families overcome obstacles—whether community support networks, targeted financial products, or effective educational programs—can inform strategies for increasing homeownership among all Black families.

3. Housing Affordability in California

California's housing market represents an extreme version of the affordability challenges facing Black families nationwide, where even modest homes require incomes far exceeding what most Black households earn. The state's unique combination of high housing costs, limited supply, and persistent income disparities creates barriers to Black homeownership that have actually worsened over recent decades despite legislative efforts to promote equity.

Current affordability data reveals the stark reality facing Black Californians seeking homeownership. As of 2024, only 10% of Black households could afford the median-priced home in California, unchanged from the previous year despite modest improvements in other economic indicators (California Association of Realtors, 2025). This compares to 21% of white households, 27% of Asian households, and 9% of Hispanic/Latino households who could afford the same median-priced home of $865,440.

The income requirements for homeownership in California have reached levels that exclude the vast majority of Black families. A minimum annual income of $221,200 was needed to qualify for a median-priced home in 2024, assuming a 20% down payment and monthly payments of $5,530 including principal, interest, and taxes (California Association of Realtors, 2025) 42 . This requirement exceeds the median income for Black households in California by more than three times, creating an affordability gap that has widened rather than narrowed over recent years.

The historical trajectory of Black homeownership in California demonstrates how discriminatory practices have created lasting disadvantages. UC Berkeley's Othering & Belonging Institute analysis shows that California's Black homeownership rate dropped from 40% to 35% between 1980 and 2020—the only racial group to experience a decline during this 40-year period (Othering & Belonging Institute, 2024).

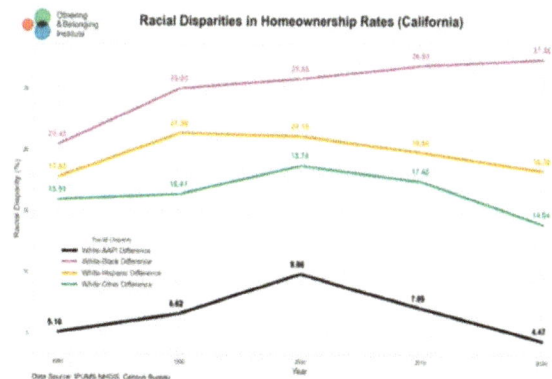

Racial Disparities in Homeownership Rates (California)

This decline occurred while other racial groups achieved historic peaks, making the relative position of Black Californians even worse over time.

Regional variations within California reveal how local economic conditions and housing costs create different challenges for Black families. The California Association of Realtors reports that counties with the largest affordability gaps between Black households and the overall population include some of the state's most expensive metropolitan areas. San Francisco, despite having a relatively smaller denial rate gap in lending, still shows significant affordability challenges due to extreme housing costs that put homeownership out of reach for most moderate-income families.

The relationship between housing costs and income growth shows how rapidly changing market conditions have outpaced Black families' capacity to achieve homeownership. California's Legislative Analyst's Office reports that monthly payments for mid-tier homes increased 82% between January 2020 and June 2025, while bottom-tier homes saw 87% increases during the same period (California Legislative Analyst's Office, 2025) 44 . These increases far exceeded wage growth of 23% during the same period, creating affordability gaps that have worsened dramatically in just five years.

Growth in Monthly Home Payments Since 2020 Driven by Both Home Prices and Mortgage Rates

Cumulative change in monthly payment for a newly purchased mid-tier home in California

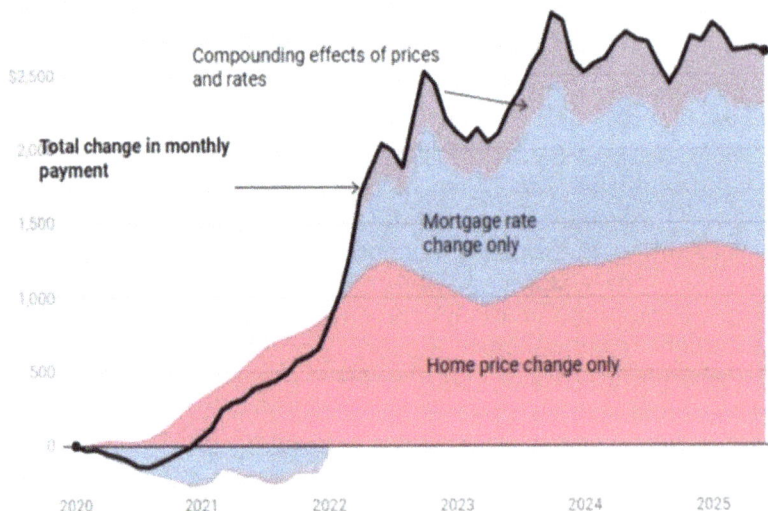

Figure 14: Growth in Monthly Home payments Since 2020 Driven by both Home Prices and Mortgage Rates. Source: California's Legislative Analyst Office, 2025.

Recent mortgage rate increases have intensified affordability challenges for all Californians but disproportionately affected Black families who typically have less wealth to cushion against higher borrowing costs. The typical monthly mortgage payment for a median-priced detached home rose 6% in 2024 compared to the previous year, while affordability for Black households remained unchanged at just 10% (PRNewswire, 2025) 45 . This suggests that Black families are being completely priced out of homeownership rather than simply facing higher costs, as even modest improvements in their economic circumstances are insufficient to overcome rapidly rising housing costs.

Down payment requirements represent a particular barrier for Black California families, who typically have less accumulated wealth and fewer family resources to draw upon.

The California Dream For All program attempted to address this barrier by providing 20% down payment assistance, but the program's $300 million in funding was exhausted in just 11 days, leaving most eligible families without support. This rapid depletion demonstrates both the enormous demand for assistance and the inadequacy of current funding levels to address the scale of need.

The concentration of Black Californians in specific metropolitan areas creates additional challenges, as these areas often have both higher housing costs and limited housing supply. Los Angeles, which houses a significant portion of California's Black population, shows a Black homeownership rate of just 33.5% despite having one of the smaller homeownership gaps nationally (Urban Institute, 2018) 36 . This reflects how absolute housing costs can overwhelm other factors that might otherwise support homeownership.

California's regulatory environment creates additional costs that can price out moderate-income families, including many Black households. The state's recent legislative efforts to streamline housing development through CEQA reform and other measures may eventually increase housing supply, but these changes will take years to significantly impact housing costs (Governor of California, 2025) 46 . In the meantime, Black families continue to face affordability challenges that worsen with each year of limited supply and increasing costs.

The interaction between rental costs and homeownership affordability creates additional pressures for Black California families. With more than half of California renters being rent-burdened (spending more than 30% of income on housing), many families struggle to save for down payments while meeting current housing costs (CalMatters, 2025) 47 . Nearly a third of Californians are severely rent-burdened (spending more than 50% of income on rent), making wealth accumulation through savings extremely difficult.

State-level initiatives to address racial homeownership disparities show both promise and limitations. California Housing Finance Agency's Building Black Wealth campaign has provided educational resources and connections to down payment assistance, while the state has funded various pilot programs aimed at increasing minority homeownership (California Housing Finance Agency, 2024) However, the scale of these programs remains small relative to the magnitude of the affordability challenge facing Black families.

Credit access and lending practices in California reflect both national patterns of discrimination and state-specific factors that may affect Black homebuyers. While California's regulatory environment may provide some protections against discriminatory lending, the high housing costs mean that even small differences in mortgage terms can have major impacts on affordability. Black families who receive slightly higher interest rates or less favorable loan terms may find themselves completely priced out of markets where white families with similar incomes can still qualify for mortgages.

The wealth impact of California's housing costs extends beyond immediate affordability to long-term wealth building opportunities. Black families who cannot access homeownership in California miss out on what has historically been the state's most reliable path to wealth accumulation, as California home values have appreciated faster than most other asset classes over long time periods. This exclusion from homeownership perpetuates and may worsen racial wealth gaps over time.

Dynamics in Homeownership

Understanding the dynamics that shape homeownership patterns requires examining how market forces, policy interventions, demographic changes, and economic cycles interact to create opportunities and barriers for different groups over time. For African American families, these dynamics have consistently produced outcomes that lag behind other racial groups, but recent years have revealed both new challenges and emerging opportunities that could reshape the trajectory of Black homeownership. The pandemic period created a unique set of dynamics that initially expanded homeownership opportunities before making them more difficult to achieve. Historic low interest rates in 2020-2021 enabled Black homeownership to gain 2 percentage points, the largest increase in decades, as families who had been marginally qualified for mortgages suddenly found themselves able to afford monthly payments on homes they previously could not purchase (Urban Wire, 2023) 32 . This period demonstrated how favorable market conditions could temporarily overcome some structural barriers to Black homeownership.

However, the rapid reversal of these conditions illustrated how fragile progress can be when underlying structural issues remain unaddressed. As the Federal Reserve raised interest rates to combat inflation, mortgage rates increased from 2.7% in January 2021 to over 7.6% by October 2023 (California Legislative Analyst's Office, 2025.

This dramatic change hit Black families particularly hard because they are more likely to be first-time buyers without existing home equity to leverage, and more likely to have limited financial reserves to weather higher monthly payments.

The inventory dynamics of housing markets create particular challenges for Black homebuyers, who often face more limited choices and greater competition for affordable homes. National Association of Realtors data shows that only 17.6% of current listings are considered affordable for the average Black household, compared to higher percentages for other racial groups (HousingWire, 2025)[40]. This scarcity forces Black families to compete more intensively for the limited affordable housing stock, often in bidding wars where cash offers and waived contingencies provide advantages that many Black families cannot match.

Generational dynamics reveal concerning trends about the future trajectory of Black homeownership. While older Black Americans achieved modest homeownership gains during favorable market conditions, younger Black Americans face steeper barriers than previous generations. Only 33% of Black millennials own homes compared to 65% of white millennials, representing the largest generational gap on record and suggesting that future Black homeownership rates may decline unless significant interventions occur.

Regional migration patterns continue to influence Black homeownership dynamics, as families seek areas with better economic opportunities, lower housing costs, or stronger community support networks.

Recent data shows some Black families moving from expensive coastal metropolitan areas to more affordable southern and western markets, potentially improving their homeownership prospects while also affecting the demographic composition of both origin and destination communities.

The wealth dynamics underlying homeownership create feedback loops that either accelerate progress or perpetuate disparities over time. Black families who successfully achieve homeownership during favorable market conditions can build equity that facilitates future real estate transactions, business investments, or support for children's homebuying efforts. Conversely, families who remain excluded from homeownership miss opportunities for wealth building that become increasingly difficult to recapture as housing costs continue rising faster than incomes.

Credit market dynamics significantly affect Black homeownership opportunities through both formal lending criteria and informal relationship-based financing. Recent research shows that Black families are more likely to rely on formal mortgage markets rather than family financing, making them more vulnerable to changes in lending standards and interest rates. When credit markets tighten or lending criteria become more stringent, Black families often experience disproportionate impacts because they have fewer alternative financing sources.

Technology dynamics are reshaping how families search for homes, apply for mortgages, and access homeownership services, with mixed implications for Black homebuyers. Online platforms can improve access to information and expand the pool of potential lenders, but algorithmic bias in automated underwriting systems may create new forms of discrimination. The COVID-19 pandemic accelerated adoption of digital mortgage processes, potentially improving efficiency but also creating new barriers for families less comfortable with digital technologies.

Policy dynamics at federal, state, and local levels create constantly shifting landscapes of opportunities and barriers for Black homeownership. Recent examples include California's efforts to streamline housing development through CEQA reform, various state down payment assistance programs, and federal initiatives like Special Purpose Credit Programs that allow lenders to provide more flexible terms for historically disadvantaged groups. However, policy implementation often lags behind policy adoption, and political changes can reverse progress before programs achieve their intended impacts.

Employment dynamics significantly affect Black homeownership through both immediate income effects and longer-term career trajectory impacts. Black workers continue to experience higher unemployment rates and greater employment volatility than white workers, making the stable income requirements for mortgage qualification more difficult to meet. Recent economic data shows some improvement in Black employment outcomes, but these gains remain vulnerable to economic downturns that historically affect Black workers more severely

Educational dynamics influence homeownership both through income effects and through the debt burdens that increasingly accompany higher education. Black college graduates carry average student loan debt of $23,420 compared to $16,046 for white graduates, creating debt-to-income ratios that can limit mortgage qualification even when education leads to higher incomes. The interaction between educational investment and homeownership capacity creates complex tradeoffs for Black families seeking economic advancement.

Community development dynamics affect Black homeownership through both the direct provision of housing opportunities and the creation of supportive environments that make homeownership more attractive and sustainable. Successful community development initiatives combine housing production with economic development, educational improvements, and public safety enhancements that increase property values and community stability over time.

Market cycle dynamics typically affect Black homeownership more severely than white homeownership during both downturns and recoveries. The 2008 financial crisis disproportionately affected Black homeowners through foreclosures and wealth destruction, and recovery from that crisis took longer for Black families than for white families. Understanding these cyclical patterns is crucial for designing policies that can provide counter-cyclical support during difficult periods while maximizing opportunities during favorable conditions.

The intersection of these various dynamics creates complex feedback effects that can either amplify or dampen the impact of individual interventions. Successful strategies for expanding Black homeownership must therefore consider how different dynamics interact and design comprehensive approaches that address multiple factors simultaneously rather than relying on single-factor solutions that may be overwhelmed by opposing forces.

Recent data suggests that the current period may represent a critical juncture for Black homeownership, with rising costs threatening to reverse pandemic-era gains while new policy tools like Special Purpose Credit Programs offer possibilities for more targeted and effective interventions. The decisions made by policymakers, lenders, and community organizations over the next few years will likely determine whether the 2020s become a decade of progress toward closing racial homeownership gaps or a period of further divergence that entrenches existing disparities for another generation.

Homeownership Trends in the Past Decade

Understanding how homeownership patterns have evolved over the past decade provides crucial context for the current disparities we seek to address through our African American Homeownership Initiative. The period from 2013 to 2023 represents a fascinating study in both progress and persistence—while overall homeownership has recovered from its Great Recession lows and minority communities have made measurable gains, the fundamental gaps between racial groups have actually widened in some disturbing ways.

The decade's trends reveal a complex narrative that defies simple characterization. On one hand, we see encouraging signs: the U.S. homeownership rate rose from 63.5% in 2013 to 65.2% in 2023, adding approximately 11.8 million new homeowners to the American landscape (National Association of Realtors, 2025) 48 . This recovery from the devastating losses of the foreclosure crisis represents genuine progress and suggests that homeownership remains an achievable goal for many American families.

Yet when we examine these trends through the lens of racial equity, the picture becomes more troubling.

While every racial group increased their homeownership rates over the decade, the benefits have been distributed so unequally that the fundamental disparities have actually intensified. The Black-white homeownership gap, which stood at 27 percentage points in 2013, expanded to 28 percentage points by 2023 despite modest gains in Black homeownership (National Association of Realtors, 2024) 30 . This means that even as more African American families achieved homeownership, white families gained access to homeownership at an even faster rate, maintaining and even expanding their advantages.

The Recovery Trajectory and Its Uneven Benefits

The homeownership recovery began before the COVID-19 pandemic but accelerated during the unprecedented period from 2020 to 2022. Understanding this trajectory helps explain both the opportunities and challenges facing prospective homeowners today. The overall homeownership rate bottomed out at 63.4% in 2016, representing a devastating 5.6 percentage point decline from the 2004 peak of 69.0% (U.S. Census Bureau, 2023) 49 . From this low point, homeownership began climbing steadily, gaining 1.2 percentage points from 2016 to 2019, and another 1.2 percentage points from 2019 to 2022.

This recovery was primarily driven by younger households, a demographic shift with significant implications for long-term homeownership patterns. From 2016 to 2022, homeownership among adults under age 55 increased substantially while remaining stable among older populations. The largest gains occurred among householders under age 35, who saw their homeownership rate increase by 2.2 percentage points from 2016 to 2019, followed by another 2 percentage point increase from 2019 to 2022 (U.S. Census Bureau, 2023) 52 . This younger buyer influx suggests that the fundamental desire for homeownership remains strong among emerging generations, despite the affordability challenges they face.

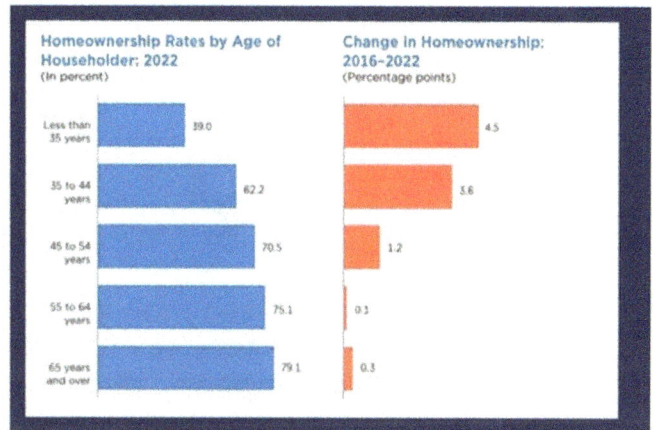

Figure 15: Younger Householders Fueled Homeownership Increase. Source: The U.S. Census Bureau, 2023.

However, the pandemic period's unique conditions—including record-low mortgage rates, increased remote work flexibility, and government stimulus payments—created an artificial boost that may not be sustainable. Mortgage rates fell to historic lows below 3% in 2020 and 2021, enabling many families to qualify for larger loans and making homeownership temporarily more accessible. As rates rose sharply in 2022 and 2023, reaching levels above 7% by late 2023, this artificial boost began to fade, creating new challenges for potential homebuyers.

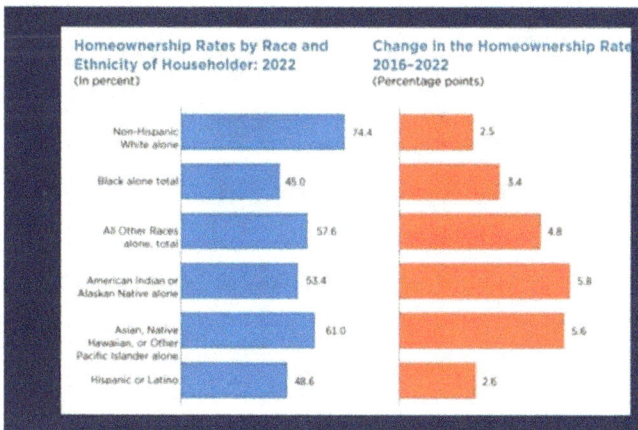

Figure 15: Homeownership Increased Among All Racial/Ethnic Groups. Source: The U.S. Census Bureau, 2023.

Racial Patterns in Homeownership Growth

While every racial and ethnic group increased their homeownership rates over the decade, the distribution of gains reveals persistent structural inequalities that our initiative seeks to address. Hispanic Americans experienced the most pronounced homeownership rate increase, gaining 5.8 percentage points to reach 51.1%, representing an addition of 3.5 million homeowners—the largest numerical increase of any racial group. Asian Americans achieved the second-largest proportional gains with a 5.6 percentage point increase to 63.3%, adding 1.6 million homeowners and reaching record-high homeownership rates.

These substantial gains for Hispanic and Asian communities demonstrate that homeownership growth is possible even within the current challenging market conditions. Hispanic households benefited from demographic advantages including younger median age (31 years) and growing household formation, with one in three Hispanic households falling into the prime homebuying age range of 25-40 years (National Association of Hispanic Real Estate Professionals, 2024) 50 . Asian households aged 25-40 increased by 34% since 2013, providing a large pool of potential homebuyers with typically higher median incomes and savings rates

In contrast, African American homeownership growth lagged significantly behind other groups. While Black homeownership increased by 2.8 percentage points from 2013 to 2023, adding nearly 1.2 million homeowners, this represented the smallest proportional gain among all racial groups (National Association of Realtors, 2025) 30 . More concerning, some recent analyses suggest that Black homeownership may have actually declined in certain regions and time periods within the decade.

Local Housing Solutions' analysis of homeownership trends from 2012 to 2022 found that while Asian and Hispanic households experienced modest growth over this slightly different timeframe, Black households actually experienced a decline of two percentage points (Local Housing Solutions, 2024) 51 . The largest declines occurred in the Midwest, where the Black homeownership rate dropped by nearly three percentage points—the steepest decline in any region. This regional variation underscores how national statistics can mask significant local challenges that require targeted intervention.

Figure 17: Percentage Point Change in Homeownership Rates by Race (2012 - 2022). Sources: American Community Survey (2008-2012, 2018-2022) via IPUMS USA, NYU Furman Center.

The Persistence of Generational Patterns

One of the most significant findings from the past decade's trends is how homeownership patterns have become increasingly stratified not just by race, but by age and generational cohort.

HOUSING MARKET GROWTH BY RACE AND ETHNICITY

Share of households, household formation and owner-household growth (2023-2024)

	SHARE OF HOUSEHOLDS OVERALL	SHARE OF NET HOUSEHOLD FORMATION GROWTH	SHARE OF NET HOMEOWNERSHIP GROWTH
Hispanic	15.2%	43.3%	35.0%
Non-Hispanic White	63.6%	17.8%	22.2%
Non-Hispanic Black	13.1%	20.0%	20.3%
Other/Two or More Races (Non-Hispanic)	8.2%	19.0%	22.4%
All Minorities	36.4%	82.3%	77.6%

Source: U.S. Census Bureau, Current Population Survey/Housing Vacancy Survey. Table 6. Homeownership Rates by Race and Ethnicity, 2024 annual averages.

Figure 16: HOUSING MARKET GROWTH BY RACE AND ETHNICITY . Source: NAHREP STATE OF HISPANIC HOMEOWNERSHIP REPORT, 2024.

These patterns have profound implications for understanding and addressing racial homeownership gaps because they reveal how historical disadvantages compound over time.

White households maintained homeownership rates around 73-74% throughout the decade, representing remarkable stability even during periods of economic uncertainty. This stability reflects the multigenerational nature of white homeownership advantages—when economic conditions improve, white families can draw upon family wealth, inherited property equity, and established credit relationships to maintain homeownership access. When conditions deteriorate, these same advantages provide buffers against homeownership loss.

For African American households, the homeownership journey remains more precarious across all age groups. Even among Black Americans with higher incomes and educational achievements, homeownership rates lag substantially behind whites with similar qualifications. Recent analysis shows that Black college graduates have homeownership rates only 3.2 percentage points higher than white high school dropouts, illustrating how educational achievement alone cannot overcome structural barriers (National Association of Realtors, 2024).

This generational persistence means that young Black adults today face compound disadvantages. Not only must they overcome the same structural barriers that have historically limited Black homeownership, but they also lack the family wealth and property inheritance that often facilitate homeownership transitions for young white adults. Research indicates that 86.4% of Black college students carry student loan debt compared to lower rates for other groups, creating additional obstacles to accumulating down payment funds (National Association of Realtors, 2024)

Regional Variations and Geographic Mobility

The past decade's homeownership trends also reveal significant regional variations that help explain national patterns and point toward local solutions. The recovery in homeownership rates occurred in all regions from 2019 to 2022, but the gains were distributed unevenly geographically and racially.

The Midwest achieved the highest regional homeownership rate at 70% by 2022, representing substantial recovery from foreclosure crisis losses (U.S. Census Bureau, 2023)

However, this regional success masked significant racial disparities within Midwest communities. While Asian and Hispanic households in the Midwest experienced homeownership gains of roughly three percentage points, Black households in the same region saw their homeownership rates decline by nearly three percentage points.

These diverging regional outcomes reflect different migration and settlement patterns among racial groups. Many Black residents have departed former industrial hubs like Detroit, Cleveland, and St. Louis due to economic disinvestment and limited opportunities, often relocating to Southern metropolitan areas with more robust job growth but also higher housing costs. Meanwhile, Asian and Hispanic households may be drawn to Midwest communities by relatively affordable housing costs and growing employment opportunities in technology, healthcare, and other expanding sectors.

The South maintained the second-highest homeownership rate at 67.3%, but this regional average encompasses enormous variation between states and metropolitan areas. Southern states like Mississippi (57%), South Carolina (55%), and Delaware (55%) showed some of the highest Black homeownership rates in the nation, while still maintaining substantial gaps compared to white homeownership in the same states (National Association of Realtors, 2024) 30 . These higher rates reflect both more affordable housing costs and historical settlement patterns, but they coexist with persistent segregation and limited wealth accumulation opportunities.

The COVID-19 Pandemic's Temporary Boost

The period from 2020 to 2022 represents a unique chapter in homeownership trends that provides both lessons and warnings for future policy development. The pandemic created unusual economic conditions that temporarily boosted homeownership across all racial groups, but these gains may prove difficult to sustain as conditions normalize.

Record-low mortgage rates, averaging below 3% for most of 2020 and 2021, dramatically improved affordability calculations for potential homebuyers. Combined with expanded unemployment benefits, stimulus payments, and increased remote work flexibility, these conditions created a brief window of opportunity that many previously excluded families used to achieve homeownership. Black homeownership increased by 2 percentage points from 2019 to 2021, the largest two-year gain in decades (Eye on Housing, 2024).

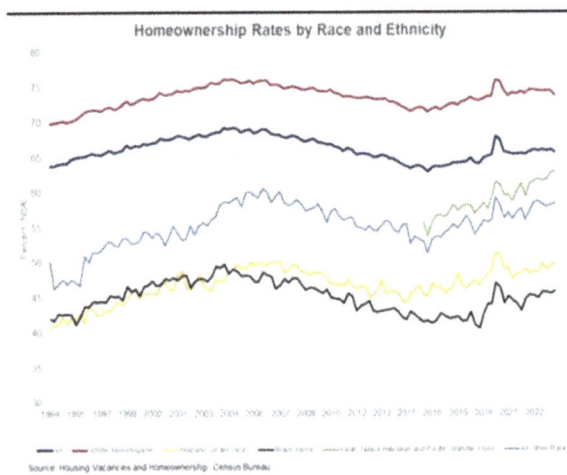

Figure 18: Homeownership Rates by Race and Ethnicity . Source: National Association of Home Builders Eye on Housing, 2024.

As mortgage rates rose sharply in 2022 and 2023, reaching over 7% by late 2023, the combination of high prices and high rates severely constrained affordability. The number of Black renter households able to afford a median-priced home fell by 39% between 2022 and 2024, compared to a 35% decline for white renters (National Association of Realtors, 2024) 30 . This suggests that the pandemic-era gains in Black homeownership may be difficult to sustain and expand under more typical market conditions.

Emerging Challenges and Future Outlook

As we look toward the future from our current vantage point in 2025, several trends from the past decade provide both warnings and opportunities for homeownership policy development. The most concerning trend is the apparent widening of racial homeownership gaps despite overall progress in homeownership recovery.

However, this pandemic-era boost came at a cost that continues to affect the housing market today. Increased buyer demand, constrained housing supply due to construction delays, and supply chain disruptions drove home prices to historic highs. The median home price increased from approximately $320,000 in early 2020 to over $420,000 by 2022, representing a 30% increase that far outpaced income growth (National Association of Realtors, 2024).

The Black-white homeownership gap of 28 percentage points in 2023 represents not just a persistent disparity but an actively worsening one. This gap is now larger than it was in the early 1990s and approaching levels not seen since the 1960s (Urban Institute, 2019) 52 . More alarming, this gap exists despite significant policy intervention including fair housing enforcement, expanded access to credit, and numerous down payment assistance programs. The persistence and expansion of the gap suggests that current approaches, while beneficial, are insufficient to address the scale and complexity of structural barriers.

Yet the decade also demonstrates that rapid homeownership gains are possible under the right conditions. Hispanic Americans added 3.5 million homeowners over the decade, Asian Americans reached record-high homeownership rates, and even Black homeownership made modest gains despite systemic barriers. These successes provide templates for understanding what works and how success might be scaled and sustained.

The decade's trends also highlight the crucial importance of addressing homeownership sustainability, not just initial access. Research from the past decade shows that households of color, particularly Black and Hispanic families, are more likely to live in homes with moderate or severe housing adequacy problems, including roof, mold, and heating issues (Local Housing Solutions, 2024) 51 . These quality issues threaten homeownership sustainability and suggest that comprehensive approaches must address ongoing homeownership support, not just initial purchase assistance.

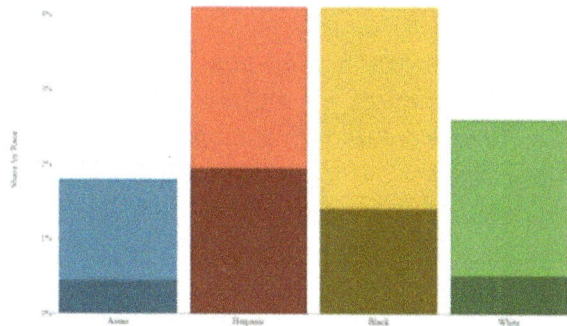

Figure 19: Share of Moderately and Severely Inadequate Homes by Race (2021). Source: Sources: American Community Survey (2008-2012, 2018-2022) via IPUMS USA, NYU Furman Center.

Looking forward, demographic trends provide both opportunities and challenges. The growing Hispanic population, with its younger age profile and increasing household formation, represents a significant driver of future housing demand. Asian households continue to show strong homeownership aspirations and typically have financial profiles that facilitate homeownership access. However, African American households face compound challenges including an aging population in some regions, continued migration patterns that may move families from affordable to expensive markets, and persistent wealth gaps that limit homeownership sustainability.

The past decade's homeownership trends thus provide a complex foundation for understanding current challenges and future opportunities. While overall homeownership recovery demonstrates that progress is possible, racial disparities have persisted and in some cases worsened. This pattern underscores the need for targeted, sustained intervention like our African American Homeownership Initiative, while also providing lessons about what approaches have succeeded and failed in different contexts and communities.

Housing Affordability by Race

Housing affordability represents the most immediate and measurable barrier separating racial groups from equal homeownership opportunities.

While discrimination and information gaps create important obstacles, affordability constraints provide the most direct explanation for why homeownership gaps persist and have widened even as overall economic conditions improved. The latest data from 2024 and 2025 reveals affordability disparities so severe that they threaten to permanently entrench racial homeownership gaps unless addressed through comprehensive intervention.

Understanding housing affordability by race requires examining not just the cost of housing, but the complex interaction between housing prices, household incomes, credit access, and wealth accumulation that determines whether families can afford not just to purchase homes, but to sustain homeownership over time. Current affordability data reveals that we have entered a period of unprecedented constraint, with affordability challenges affecting even middle-class households while falling most heavily on communities of color.

National Affordability Crisis with Disproportionate Racial Impact

The scale of America's current housing affordability crisis provides essential context for understanding racial disparities. According to the National Association of Home Builders' 2025 analysis, 76.4 million households—57% of all American households—cannot afford a $300,000 home using conventional underwriting standards that assume housing costs should not exceed 28% of household income (National Association of Home Builders, 2025) 53 . Even more striking, 75% of all households cannot afford the median-priced new home of $459,826 based on current mortgage rates of 6.5%.

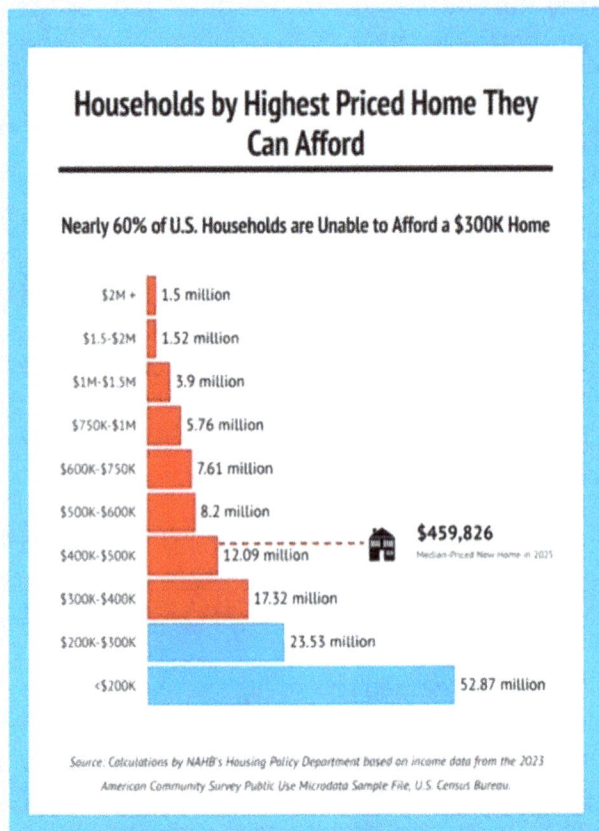

Households by Highest Priced Home They Can Afford

Nearly 60% of U.S. Households are Unable to Afford a $300K Home

$2M +	1.5 million
$1.5-$2M	1.52 million
$1M-$1.5M	3.9 million
$750K-$1M	5.76 million
$600K-$750K	7.61 million
$500K-$600K	8.2 million
$400K-$500K	12.09 million
$300K-$400K	17.32 million
$200K-$300K	23.53 million
<$200K	52.87 million

$459,826
Median-Priced New Home in 2025

Source: Calculations by NAHB's Housing Policy Department based on income data from the 2023 American Community Survey Public Use Microdata Sample File, U.S. Census Bureau.

Figure 20: Nearly 60% of U.S. Households Unable to Afford a $300K Home. Source: Calculations by NAHB's Housing Policy department based on Income data from 2023 American Community Survey Public Use Microdata Sample File, U.S. Census Bureau

These national statistics, while alarming, significantly understate the affordability challenges facing households of color. When we disaggregate affordability data by race, the disparities become stark and help explain the persistent homeownership gaps we examined in the previous chapter. Only 9% of Black renter households and 9% of Hispanic/Latino households can afford to purchase a median-priced existing home, compared to 21% of white households and 27% of Asian households (California Association of Realtors, 2024).

CALIFORNIA ASSOCIATION OF REALTORS®
2024 Traditional Housing Affordability Index by Ethnicity

2024	C.A.R. Traditional Housing Affordability Index							
STATE/REGION/COUNTY	All	White Non-Hispanic	Asian	Hispanic/Latino	Black	Median Home Price	Monthly Payment Including Taxes & Insurance	Minimum Qualifying Income
Calif. Single-family home	18	21	27	9	10	$865,440	$5,530	$221,200
Calif. Condo/Townhome	27	32	38	16	16	$675,000	$4,310	$172,400
United States	38	41	54	32	24	$412,500	$2,630	$105,200

Figure 21: CALIFORNIA ASSOCIATION OF REALTORS® 2024 Traditional Housing Affordability Index by Ethnicity Source: California Association of Realtors, 2024.

These affordability ratios translate into vastly different homeownership opportunities across racial lines. A white renter household is more than twice as likely as a Black renter household to have the income necessary for homeownership. An Asian household is three times as likely as a Black household to meet basic affordability requirements. These disparities exist even before considering other barriers such as credit scores, debt-to-income ratios, and down payment requirements that may further limit access for communities of color.

The income requirements for homeownership have risen dramatically in recent years, creating affordability barriers that disproportionately affect households of color. In California, which provides detailed affordability analysis by ethnicity, a minimum annual income of $221,200 was needed to qualify for the purchase of the $865,440 statewide median-priced existing single-family home in 2024 (California Association of Realtors, 2024) 43 . This income requirement has profound implications for racial equity because median household incomes vary so dramatically by race.

Income Disparities That Drive Affordability Gaps

The foundation of racial affordability disparities lies in persistent income inequalities that reflect the legacy of discrimination and limited access to wealth-building opportunities

Current income data reveals gaps so substantial that equal homeownership access would be impossible even if all other barriers were eliminated.

In California, the 2023 median income showed significant racial disparities: whites earned $103,870, Asians earned $120,630, Hispanics/Latinos earned $75,950, and Blacks earned $63,800 (California Association of Realtors, 2024) 43 . These income gaps represent more than economic differences—they reflect the compounding effects of historical discrimination, educational disparities, occupational segregation, and limited access to high-paying career paths.

To understand the magnitude of these income disparities, consider that the Black median income of $63,800 falls nearly $157,400 short of the $221,200 required to purchase a median-priced California home. This means that the typical Black household would need to more than triple their income to achieve basic homeownership affordability, while the typical Asian household earning $120,630 would need to increase their income by approximately 83%. Even the white median income of $103,870 falls more than $117,000 short of homeownership affordability requirements.

Nationally, similar income disparities persist across regions and metropolitan areas. The latest data shows Black workers earn approximately 82% of white worker earnings, with median weekly earnings of $1,000 compared to $1,219 for white workers (Economic Policy Institute, 2024) 5 . Over a full year, this weekly difference of $219 compounds into over $11,000 less annual income for full-time Black workers. When applied to mortgage qualification calculations that typically require housing costs to remain below 28% of gross income, this income gap translates directly into dramatically different housing budgets and homeownership opportunities.

Wages for select demographic groups, 1979, 2019, and 2024 (2024$)

50th percentile wage	1979	2019	2024	Annualized percent change 1979–2019	2019–2024
All	$19.29	$23.52	$24.87	0.5%	1.1%
Male	$24.23	$25.48	$26.90	0.1%	1.1%
Female	$15.28	$21.54	$22.90	0.9%	1.2%
White	$19.97	$25.84	$27.28	0.6%	1.1%
Black	$16.66	$19.69	$21.40	0.4%	1.7%
Hispanic	$16.37	$19.07	$20.34	0.4%	1.3%
AAPI		$29.35	$31.35		1.3%
Race/ethnicity and gender					
White women	$15.49	$23.33	$24.78	1.0%	1.2%
White men	$25.43	$28.86	$29.89	0.3%	0.7%
Black women	$14.47	$19.05	$20.80	0.7%	1.8%
Black men	$19.20	$20.37	$22.13	0.1%	1.7%
Hispanic women	$13.52	$18.01	$19.53	0.7%	1.6%
Hispanic men	$18.85	$20.51	$21.76	0.2%	1.2%
Age					
16–24	$13.66	$14.66	$16.66	0.2%	2.6%
25+	$22.33	$25.46	$27.01	0.3%	1.2%
Education					
Less than a four-year degree	$18.25	$19.08	$20.13	0.1%	1.1%
Bachelor's degree or higher	$28.05	$36.09	$37.32	0.6%	0.7%

Note: AAPI refers to Asian American and Pacific Islander. Race/ethnicity categories are mutually exclusive (i.e., white non-Hispanic, Black non-Hispanic, AAPI non-Hispanic, and Hispanic any race).

Source: EPI analysis of the Current Population Survey Outgoing Rotation Group microdata. EPI Current Population Survey Extracts, Version 1.0.61 (2025a). https://microdata.epi.org

Economic Policy Institute

Figure 22. Wages for select demographic groups, 1979, 2019, and 2024 (2024$). Source: Economic Policy Institute, 2024.

The intersection of race and gender compounds these income disparities in ways that particularly affect Black women, who represent a significant portion of potential homebuyers. Black women earn 89.2% of white women's earnings but face additional challenges related to higher rates of single parenthood and student loan debt that further constrain their homeownership opportunities (Economic Policy Institute, 2024) 59 . These intersectional disparities help explain why targeted programs like our African American Homeownership Initiative must address multiple, compound barriers simultaneously.

Regional Variations in Affordability Patterns

While affordability challenges affect communities of color nationwide, the severity and specific nature of these challenges vary significantly by region and metropolitan area. Understanding these geographic variations provides insight into both the scope of needed intervention and potential strategies for addressing affordability barriers.

California represents an extreme case that illustrates national trends in concentrated form. The state's housing affordability crisis affects all racial groups but falls most heavily on Black and Hispanic households. Housing affordability for white households in California fell from 25% in 2022 to 21% in 2023, while only 9% of Black households could afford the same median-priced home, down from 11% the previous year (California Association of Realtors, 2024) 58 . These figures mean that even as overall affordability declined, the racial gaps actually widened.

The affordability gap between Black households and the overall population in California did show some improvement, narrowing from 9.7 percentage points in 2022 to 8.5 percentage points in 2023, while the gap for Hispanic/Latino households improved from 9.4 to 8.3 percentage points (California Association of Realtors, 2024). However, these gap improvements resulted primarily from declining affordability for all groups rather than from improved access for communities of color.

Different metropolitan areas within California show varying levels of affordability challenge, providing insight into how local conditions affect racial homeownership opportunities. The counties with the largest affordability gaps between Black and overall populations in 2023 were Contra Costa (15%), San Francisco (15%), and Fresno (13%) counties (California Association of Realtors, 2024). These large gaps suggest that even within the same state, local housing markets, employment opportunities, and historical settlement patterns create different levels of barriers for communities of color.

At the national level, affordability challenges vary significantly by region, but racial disparities persist across all geographic areas. The NAHB/Wells Fargo Cost of Housing Index shows that in the first quarter of 2025, a typical family needed to spend 35% of their income for a median-priced existing home, while low-income families (earning 50% of median income) would need to spend 70% of their earnings for the same home (National Association of Home Builders, 2025). However, because median incomes vary dramatically by race, these "typical family" statistics mask the much more severe constraints facing households of color.

The Compounding Effect of Wealth Disparities

Income differences, while substantial, represent only part of the affordability challenge facing communities of color. Wealth disparities—the accumulated assets that families can draw upon for down payments, closing costs, and ongoing homeownership expenses—create additional layers of affordability constraint that pure income measures fail to capture.

The Federal Reserve's 2022 Survey of Consumer Finances revealed that Black families hold a median wealth of $44,900, representing only 15.7% of white family wealth of $285,000 (Federal Reserve, 2023). This wealth gap means that even Black families with sufficient income to qualify for mortgages often lack the accumulated assets necessary for homeownership transition.

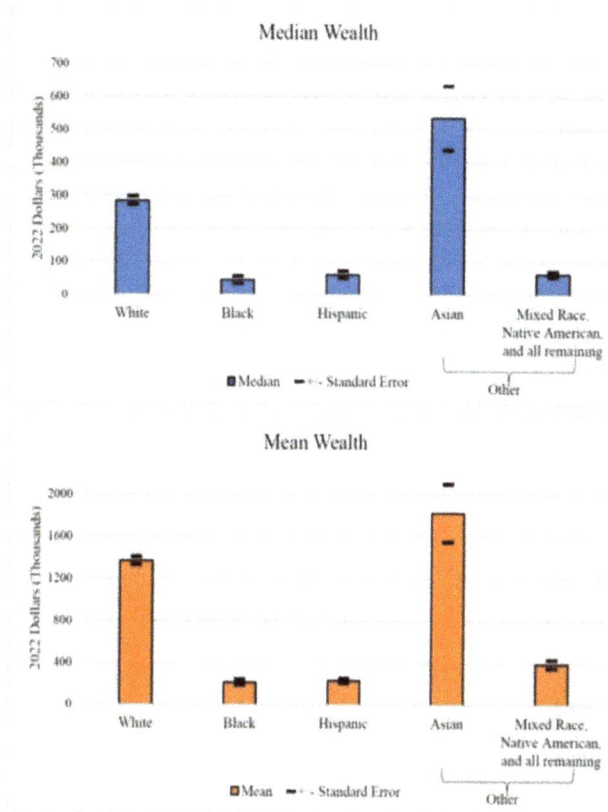

Figure 23. White and Asian Families Had the Most Wealth. Source: Source: Board of Governors of the Federal Reserve System (2023).

Consider the practical implications of this wealth disparity for homeownership affordability. A typical home purchase requires not just sufficient income to qualify for a mortgage, but also cash for down payments (typically 3-20% of purchase price), closing costs (typically 2-5% of purchase price), moving expenses, immediate repairs and improvements, and reserves for ongoing maintenance and emergency expenses. For a $300,000 home, these upfront costs can easily total $25,000-75,000, amounts that exceed the total median wealth of Black families.

This wealth constraint helps explain why only 8% of Black renter households have at least $20,000 in cash savings available for down payments, compared to 18% of white renters (National Association of Realtors, 2024) 30 . The absence of accumulated wealth means that even Black families with sufficient income for mortgage payments cannot access homeownership opportunities, creating what economists call "wealth-constrained demand" that income-focused affordability measures fail to identify.

The wealth gap also affects homeownership sustainability and wealth-building potential once families do achieve homeownership. Black homeowners typically carry higher debt-to-income ratios and have less financial cushion for unexpected expenses, making them more vulnerable to foreclosure during economic downturns or personal financial crises. Additionally, Black homeowners are more likely to live in neighborhoods with limited appreciation potential, constraining their ability to build wealth through homeownership.

Cost Burden Analysis by Race

Understanding how housing costs affect different racial groups requires examining not just homeownership affordability, but also the cost burdens experienced by current homeowners and renters. This analysis reveals how affordability constraints persist even after homeownership is achieved and helps explain why homeownership sustainability requires ongoing attention.

Recent Census Bureau analysis of housing cost burdens by race reveals significant disparities in the share of income dedicated to housing expenses. Among Black renter households, 56.2% are cost-burdened (spending more than 30% of income on housing), with 30.6% severely cost-burdened (spending more than 50% of income on housing) (U.S. Census Bureau, 2024) 55 . Hispanic households experience similar constraints, with 53.2% cost-burdened and 28.8% severely cost-burdened.

These cost burden disparities affect not just current living conditions but also future homeownership opportunities. Renter households spending more than 30% of their income on rent have limited ability to save for down payments or build the credit history necessary for mortgage qualification. Those spending more than 50% of income on housing often face monthly financial stress that prevents any wealth accumulation.

For current homeowners, cost burden disparities persist and help explain homeownership sustainability challenges. Black homeowners experience higher housing cost burdens in 39 states, spending more than 30% of their income on housing costs (National Association of Realtors, 2025).This cost burden affects homeowners' ability to maintain their properties, build equity through additional payments, or weather financial emergencies without risking foreclosure

The persistence of cost burdens among homeowners of color also reflects the types of mortgages and homes accessible to families with limited wealth and constrained credit access. Black and Hispanic homeowners are more likely to carry higher-interest loans, have less favorable loan terms, and live in areas with higher property taxes relative to property values. They also face higher homeowners insurance costs, with Black homeowners paying more for insurance than any other group (National Association of Realtors, 2025).

Credit and Lending Access Disparities

Housing affordability extends beyond income and wealth to encompass access to credit and favorable lending terms. Even families with sufficient income and savings may face affordability barriers if they cannot access mortgages or receive less favorable interest rates that increase their monthly payments and total homeownership costs.

Current mortgage denial rates reveal persistent disparities that affect affordability even for qualified borrowers. Black applicants face denial rates of 17-24%, compared to 5.8-11% for white applicants—meaning Black applicants are nearly three times as likely to be denied mortgage approval (Consumer Financial Protection Bureau, 2024) 8 . Hispanic applicants face denial rates of 15-19%, while Asian applicants experience denial rates similar to whites at 9-10%.

These differential denial rates mean that Black and Hispanic families must often seek alternative financing that carries higher costs, accept less favorable loan terms, or delay homeownership while addressing credit issues. Each of these responses increases the effective cost of homeownership and creates additional affordability barriers beyond those captured in standard income-to-housing-cost ratios.

For Black and Hispanic applicants who do receive mortgage approval, the terms are often less favorable than those offered to white applicants with similar financial profiles. Recent NAR data shows that 20% of mortgages for Black borrowers and 21% for Hispanic borrowers had interest rates exceeding 6%, compared to 18% for white borrowers and 15% for Asian borrowers (National Association of Realtors, 2024) 51 . These rate differentials of 0.1-0.3 percentage points may seem small but compound over the life of a 30-year mortgage into thousands of dollars in additional costs.

The Affordability Crisis's Future Trajectory

Current affordability data provides a foundation for understanding not just present challenges but also future trends that will affect racial homeownership gaps over the coming decade. Several factors suggest that affordability constraints may intensify unless addressed through comprehensive intervention.

House price growth continues to outpace income growth across all racial groups, but the impact falls most heavily on communities of color with lower baseline incomes and limited wealth accumulation. The national house price-to-income ratio reached 130 index points in 2024, meaning that housing costs have grown 30% faster than incomes since the 2015 baseline (Statista, 2024) 56 . For communities of color starting from lower income levels, this price-to-income divergence creates increasingly insurmountable barriers to homeownership access.

Interest rate projections suggest that mortgage costs will remain elevated compared to the historic lows of 2020-2021, maintaining affordability pressure for potential homebuyers. Even if rates decline modestly from current levels above 7%, they are unlikely to return to the sub-4% levels that enabled many pandemic-era homeownership gains. This means that future homeownership growth will need to rely more heavily on income growth and targeted assistance rather than favorable interest rate conditions.

Demographic trends provide both challenges and opportunities for addressing racial affordability disparities. The Hispanic population's younger age profile and continued household formation create a growing pool of potential homebuyers, but they also increase demand pressure that may drive prices higher. The aging of the overall population may eventually free up housing stock as older homeowners downsize or relocate, but this process typically occurs slowly and may not benefit communities of color if the released housing is in areas with limited minority presence.

Housing supply constraints continue to limit affordability improvement across all markets and racial groups. Despite decades of discussion about increasing housing production, most metropolitan areas continue to experience housing shortages that drive prices above levels that moderate-income families can afford. Without substantial increases in housing supply, affordability improvements for communities of color will require either dramatic income increases or substantial public intervention through down payment assistance, favorable lending programs, and other targeted supports.

The housing affordability crisis by race thus represents both the most immediate barrier to homeownership equity and the most complex challenge to address. Affordability constraints result from the intersection of income disparities, wealth gaps, credit access limitations, and housing market conditions that have developed over decades and cannot be quickly reversed. However, understanding these constraints also provides a roadmap for targeted intervention through programs like our African American Homeownership Initiative that address multiple barriers simultaneously and provide the comprehensive support necessary for families to achieve and sustain homeownership in an increasingly challenging market.

Black Homeownership in 2025: Progress Amid Persistent Barriers

The landscape of African American homeownership in 2024-2025 reflects both promising developments and persistent challenges that continue to shape housing equity across the United States. While our earlier analysis established the fundamental barriers that have historically limited Black homeownership, understanding current market dynamics provides crucial context for both the opportunities and obstacles that African American families face today. These trends reveal how macroeconomic forces, demographic shifts, and policy interventions intersect to create a complex environment where progress coexists with enduring disparities.

Recent data illuminates a market characterized by contradictions. On one hand, the National Association of Realtors reports that Black homeownership experienced the greatest year-over-year increase among racial groups in 2023, representing meaningful momentum in closing longstanding gaps (National Association of Realtors, 2025) 50 . On the other hand, this progress occurs within a housing market that remains fundamentally challenging for all buyers, with elevated mortgage rates, limited inventory, and persistent affordability constraints creating additional hurdles for African American families who typically have lower household incomes and less accumulated wealth.

The significance of understanding these current trends extends beyond academic interest. For organizations like The Power Is Now Media Inc. and the communities we serve, current market conditions directly influence the effectiveness of homeownership initiatives and the strategic approaches most likely to succeed. When mortgage denial rates for Black applicants reach 19% compared to 11.27% for all applicants—representing a 1.7 times higher likelihood of denial—the urgency of targeted intervention becomes clear (Mortgage Professional, 2025).

This analysis examines four critical aspects of the current homeownership environment: the state of mortgage applications from Black families, the demographic composition and diversity of potential homebuyers, the impact of record-low housing inventory on access and affordability, and the specific opportunities for growth that current conditions create. Each element reveals both the challenges that must be addressed and the pathways that can lead to expanded Black homeownership.

Mortgage Applications from Black Families

The mortgage application and approval process represents the most direct gateway to homeownership, making trends in this area particularly significant for understanding access barriers. Current data reveals a troubling picture of persistent discrimination and systemic barriers that continue to limit African American families' access to homeownership financing, despite decades of fair lending legislation and regulatory oversight.

Current Denial Rate Disparities present the most stark evidence of ongoing challenges. According to the most recent LendingTree analysis of Home Mortgage Disclosure Act data, Black homebuyers faced a nationwide mortgage denial rate of 19% in 2024, compared to 11.27% for all applicants (Scotsman Guide, 2025) 59 . This 1.7 times higher likelihood of denial represents a slight improvement from the 1.8 times disparity observed in previous years, but the absolute gap of 7.73 percentage points remains substantial and economically significant.

Year	Denial rate, all borrowers	Denial rate, Black borrowers	Spread
2024	9.47%	14.27%	4.80
2022	9.14%	14.44%	5.30

Table 2: Mortgage denial rates across 50 largest metros: All buyers vs. Black buyers. Source: LendingTree analysis of 2024 Home Mortgage Disclosure Act (HMDA) data.

The geographic variation in these denial rates reveals particularly concerning patterns. Grand Rapids, Michigan, shows the highest denial rate for Black applicants at 23.9%, followed by Detroit at 21.3%, and Miami with similarly elevated rates (LendingTree, 2025) 60 . These metros experience denial rate gaps of 9.75, 8.54, and similar differentials respectively, indicating that certain markets present especially challenging environments for Black homebuyers. Conversely, Salt Lake City shows the smallest gap with Black denial rates only 0.24 points higher than overall rates, suggesting that market-specific factors significantly influence lending disparities.

Metro	Denial rate, Black borrowers, 2022	Denial rate, Black borrowers, 2024	% change
Grand Rapids, MI	21.58%	23.90%	10.75%
Detroit, MI	19.45%	21.25%	9.25%
Raleigh, NC	15.47%	16.41%	6.08%

Table 3: % change in denial rates for Black borrowers among metros with biggest spreads. Source: LendingTree analysis of 2024 Home Mortgage Disclosure Act (HMDA) data

Reason Code Analysis provides insight into the stated justifications for mortgage denials and reveals important patterns. Debt-to-income ratio represents the most common denial reason across all racial groups, accounting for 34.02% of denials overall and 34.08% among Black applicants. However, credit history emerges as a disproportionate barrier for African American applicants, representing the primary reason for 33.16% of Black denials compared to 24.85% of all denials—an 8.31 percentage point gap.

This credit history disparity reflects deeper structural issues in credit access and scoring systems. Research indicates that 33% of Black households have thin credit files insufficient for generating credit scores, compared to only 18% of white households (National Community Reinvestment Coalition, 2021) 61 . The recent announcement by Federal Housing Finance Agency Director Bill Pulte that Fannie Mae and Freddie Mac will begin allowing VantageScore 4.0 for mortgage credit checks may help address this disparity, as VantageScore incorporates rent payment data that often benefits Black and Hispanic borrowers who have been excluded from traditional credit systems.

Share of Households with a Mortgage by FICO Score, 2016

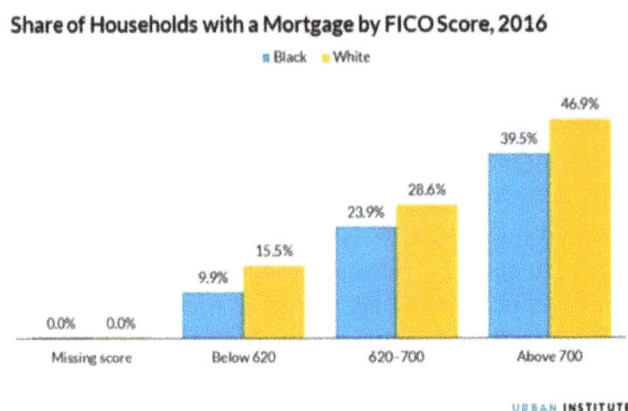

Figure 24. Share of Households with a Mortgage by Fico Score. Source: Urban Institute, 2020.

Federal Reserve Research Findings provide additional context that raises questions about the legitimacy of these denial disparities. The Federal Reserve Bank of Minneapolis conducted a comprehensive study using confidential HMDA data that included full credit scores and found that lender-reported denial reasons do not explain racial disparities (Federal Reserve Bank of Minneapolis, 2024) 34 . Even when controlling for credit history and financial qualifications, Black applicants remained 11.6% more likely to be denied for credit history reasons and 10.0% more likely to receive "Other" as a denial reason—a category that provides no transparency about actual denial factors.

Trend Analysis reveals both concerning developments and potential areas for optimism. While denial rates have decreased across all racial groups since 2022, the Black-white gap in denial rates actually narrowed from 5.30 percentage points in 2022 to 4.80 percentage points in 2024 among the 50 largest metropolitan areas. However, when examined nationally, the gap has remained stubbornly persistent, and some analyses suggest it may be widening in certain markets.

The implications for homeownership access are profound. When nearly one in five Black mortgage applicants face denial compared to approximately one in nine applicants overall, the cumulative effect creates significant barriers to homeownership that extend beyond individual transactions. Families who experience denial often delay homebuying attempts, may seek less favorable financing alternatives, or may abandon homeownership goals entirely.

Household Age and Diversity

The demographic composition of potential homebuyers reveals both current market dynamics and future opportunities for African American homeownership. Understanding age distributions, household formation patterns, and diversity trends provides crucial insight into both the challenges facing existing homebuyers and the potential for expanding Black homeownership as demographic conditions evolve over the next decade.

Generational Distribution among current homebuyers shows important patterns that influence market dynamics. According to the National Association of Realtors' 2024 generational analysis, buyers aged 45-59 years represent one of the most racially and ethnically diverse populations of homebuyers, with 25% identifying as a race other than white/Caucasian (National Association of Realtors, 2024) 62 . This age cohort often possesses more established careers, higher incomes, and greater accumulated wealth compared to younger buyers, potentially creating opportunities for increased Black homeownership among mature households.

AGE OF HOME BUYER

	All Buyers	18 to 25	26 to 34	35 to 44	45 to 59	60 to 69	70 to 78	79 to 99
White/Caucasian	83%	79%	81%	77%	79%	85%	91%	94%
Black/African-American	7	8	7	10	10	5	3	3
Hispanic/Latino	6	9	10	8	7	5	3	2
Asian/Pacific Islander	4	5	6	7	5	3	1	2
Other	3	2	2	4	3	3	2	*

Figure 25. RACE / ETHNICITY OF HOME BUYERS. Source: NAR Home Buyers and Sellers Generational Trends, 2025.

Younger millennials (ages 26-34) and older millennials (ages 35-44) collectively represent 29% of recent homebuyers, with younger millennials making up 12% and older millennials comprising 17% of the market. Significantly, 71% of younger millennials and 36% of older millennials were first-time homebuyers, indicating that these generations continue to enter homeownership markets despite challenging conditions. For African American families, who are more likely to be first-time buyers across all age groups, understanding millennial homebuying patterns becomes particularly important.

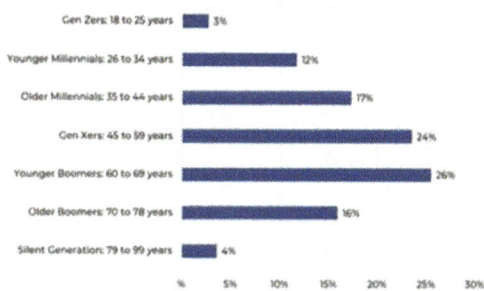

Figure 25. AGE OF HOME BUYERS. Source: NAR Home Buyers and Sellers Generational Trends, 2025.

First-Time Buyer Demographics reveal striking disparities across racial groups that illuminate both barriers and opportunities. Among first-time homebuyers specifically, 49% of Black buyers, 43% of Asian buyers, 41% of Hispanic buyers, and only 20% of white buyers are purchasing their first homes (National Association of Realtors, 2025)

This pattern reflects both the historical exclusion of minority groups from homeownership and the ongoing barriers that delay homeownership for African American families.

The high percentage of Black first-time buyers indicates that African American families often lack generational wealth transfers and family homeownership experience that facilitate homebuying for white families. However, it also suggests significant pent-up demand and market potential if barriers can be addressed effectively. When combined with demographic projections showing 1.5 million Black households approaching median homebuying age over the next five years, the opportunity for substantial growth in Black homeownership becomes apparent.

Educational and Economic Characteristics of diverse homebuyers provide additional context for market participation. Younger millennials are the most educated homebuyer group, with 78% holding bachelor's degrees or higher, yet they also enter homeownership with the lowest household incomes (National Association of Realtors, 2024) 70 . This educational achievement without corresponding income growth reflects broader economic trends that particularly affect communities of color, where educational attainment has not translated into proportional wealth accumulation

For Black homebuyers specifically, 42% report having student loan debt, up from 41% the previous year, compared to lower percentages among other racial groups. This debt burden, combined with typical first-time buyer challenges, creates compounding barriers to homeownership. Student loan payments directly affect debt-to-income ratios used in mortgage underwriting and reduce available funds for down payment savings.

Geographic and Housing Preferences among diverse buyers reveal important market dynamics. Analysis shows that minority homebuyers, particularly Black and Hispanic families, are more likely to purchase in urban areas and less likely to purchase in suburban locations compared to white buyers. This geographic concentration reflects both housing affordability constraints and historical patterns of residential segregation that continue to influence housing choice.

However, demographic trends suggest potential changes in these patterns. One in three Hispanic households fall into the 25-40 age group of prime homebuying age, with Asian households aged 25-40 increasing by 34% since 2013, and 21% more young Hispanic households in communities than a decade ago (National Association of Realtors, 2025) 50 . These demographic shifts indicate growing diversity in homebuying markets that could create opportunities for expanded access and integration.

Income and Financing Patterns reveal both barriers and adaptive strategies among diverse homebuyers. Black homebuyers utilize government and community down payment assistance programs at higher rates than other groups, with 5% using such programs compared to lower usage rates among white and Asian buyers. Additionally, 11% of Black buyers tap 401(k)/pension funds for down payments, though this percentage decreased from 17% the previous year.

The typical down payment among Black buyers remains lower than other groups, reflecting both income constraints and wealth disparities. Asian buyers maintain the highest down payments at 21%, followed by white buyers at 19%, while Black and Hispanic buyers typically make smaller down payments that require additional financing assistance or mortgage insurance. These demographic patterns underscore both the challenges facing diverse homebuyers and the significant potential for growth if appropriate support systems can be developed and implemented effectively.

Record-Low Housing Inventory

The chronic shortage of available housing inventory represents one of the most significant challenges facing all homebuyers in 2024-2025, but its impact on African American families proves particularly severe due to existing income and wealth disparities. Understanding current inventory conditions, their causes, and their differential impact on communities of color provides crucial context for developing effective homeownership strategies.

Current Inventory Levels and Trends reveal a market still struggling with severe supply constraints despite some recent improvements.

While housing inventory has shown 20 consecutive months of year-over-year growth through June 2025, current levels remain 20-30% below historical averages and well below pre-COVID conditions (Krimmel, Speianu, and Hale 2025) 63 . Existing single-family homes for sale are up roughly 20% year-over-year nationally, but absolute numbers remain near record lows, creating continued competition among buyers.

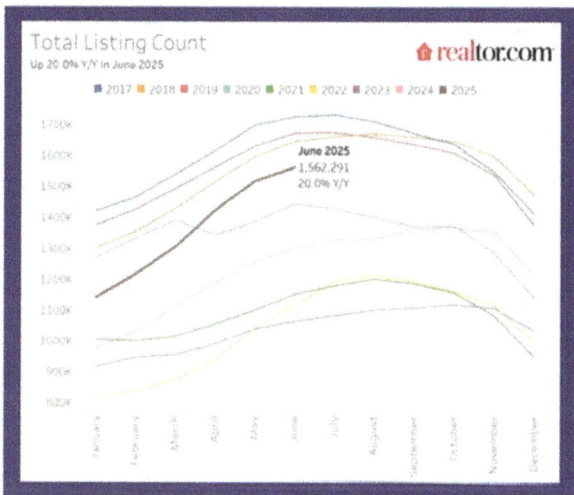

Figure 25. Total Listing Count. Source: realtor.com, 2025.

Freddie Mac's latest analysis estimates the national housing shortage at 3.7 million units as of Q3 2024, a slight improvement from their previous estimate of 3.8 million units in 2020, but still representing a massive supply deficit (Freddie Mac, 2024) 64 . This shortage affects all market segments but proves particularly challenging for first-time and moderate-income buyers who compete for a limited pool of affordable properties.

Regional Variations in inventory levels create different market dynamics across the country that significantly influence opportunities for Black homebuyers.

The South leads in addressing housing supply gaps, with projections suggesting the region could close its housing shortage in just three years at current construction rates (Newsweek, 2025) 65 . Texas alone accounted for 15% of all new-home construction permits in 2024, demonstrating the regional concentration of building activity.

In contrast, other regions face much longer timelines for addressing supply shortages. The West would require 6.5 years to close the housing gap at current construction rates, while the Midwest would need 41 years, and the Northeast may never fully address the shortage given current building patterns. These regional disparities are particularly significant for African American families, who are geographically concentrated in certain metropolitan areas and may have limited mobility to pursue opportunities in markets with better inventory conditions.

Construction and Development Challenges contribute to persistent supply shortages through multiple mechanisms. Higher costs for labor, building materials, and land have increased construction expenses, while local zoning restrictions limit development possibilities in many markets. Financing limitations, especially for multifamily projects, further constrain new supply development.

Recent data shows mixed signals in construction activity. Single-family home starts totaled 1.01 million in 2024, up 6.5% from 2023, but total housing starts decreased to 1.36 million from 1.42 million due to declining multifamily construction (Newsweek, 2025) 65 . While single-family construction has increased, the slower pace of multifamily development particularly affects rental markets and entry-level homeownership opportunities that serve diverse communities.

Policy and Economic Factors influencing inventory include both supportive measures and potential complications. Builders have recognized supply shortage problems and responded with increased construction efforts, with new home construction outpacing household formation for the first time since 2016. However, this achievement comes with concerning underlying factors: an estimated 1.6 million expected Gen Z and millennial households did not form in 2024 due to affordability constraints, meaning some of the improvement in supply-demand balance reflects reduced household formation rather than adequate housing production.

Potential policy changes under the Trump administration could significantly impact construction and inventory. Proposed tariffs on Canadian lumber could increase construction costs, while mass deportation of undocumented immigrants might create labor shortages in construction industries. Housing experts warn that these policies could reduce construction activity just as the market begins to address supply shortages.

Disproportionate Impact on African American Homebuyers manifests through several mechanisms. Limited inventory creates competitive markets where buyers with stronger financial profiles—higher incomes, larger down payments, cash purchases—have significant advantages. African American families, who typically have lower median household incomes and less accumulated wealth, face disadvantages in competitive bidding situations.

The "lock-in effect" from current homeowners holding mortgages with rates well below current market levels further constrains inventory. As of Q4 2024, 82% of homeowners with mortgages had interest rates below 6%, and this share could approach 75% by the end of 2025 (U.S. News, 2025) 66 . This dynamic particularly affects entry-level and moderately-priced homes that would be most accessible to Black first-time buyers.

Market Adaptation and New Construction Trends show builders responding to inventory constraints by increasing new home construction as a percentage of available inventory. New construction now represents approximately 30% of overall single-family detached housing inventory in recent months, more than double its typical market share (U.S. News, 2025) 74 . For African American buyers, this trend creates both opportunities and challenges: new construction offers move-in ready homes without competing against existing homeowners, but typically comes with higher price points that may exceed affordable ranges.

Opportunities for Growth

Despite the significant challenges outlined in mortgage access, demographic barriers, and inventory constraints, current market conditions and demographic trends create substantial opportunities for expanding African American homeownership. Understanding and capitalizing on these opportunities requires recognizing how changing demographics, policy innovations, and market adaptations can be leveraged to overcome historical barriers.

Demographic Momentum presents perhaps the most significant opportunity for growth in Black homeownership over the next decade. The National Association of Realtors projects that 1.5 million Black households will reach median homebuying age over the next five years, alongside 2.2 million Hispanic households and 775,000 Asian households (Newsweek, 2024) 65 . This demographic wave represents unprecedented potential for expanding minority homeownership if appropriate support systems can be developed and deployed effectively.

Recent analysis reveals that female and millennial buyers have been driving growth in Black homeownership, with female buyers experiencing 10.4% average year-over-year growth rates between 2018 and 2021, while Black millennial buyers achieved 13.8% annual growth during the same period (Xu and Hale 2022) 65 . These trends suggest that targeted programs focused on millennial families and female-headed households could yield significant results.

Policy and Program Innovations create new pathways to homeownership that specifically address historical barriers faced by African American families. The development and expansion of Special Purpose Credit Programs represents a particularly promising approach. These programs, authorized under the Equal Credit Opportunity Act of 1974, allow lenders to provide more flexible criteria and enhanced assistance to groups that have faced historical discrimination.

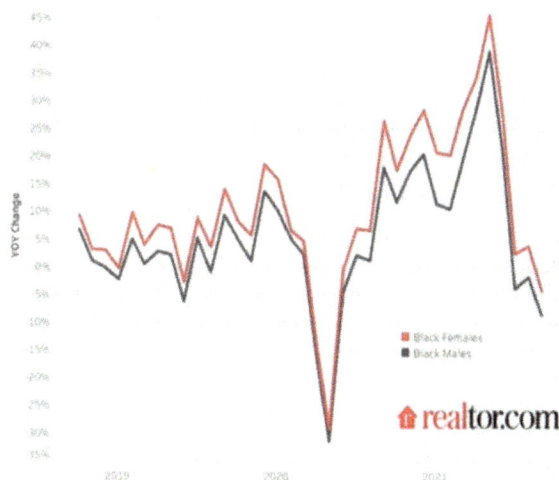

Figure 26. Black Female Homebuyers Consistently Outgrew Male Counterparts. Source: realtor.com, 2022.

Twin Cities Habitat for Humanity's Advancing Black Homeownership Program demonstrates the potential of this approach, providing up to $50,000 in down payment assistance and utilizing flexible lending criteria specifically designed for Foundational Black Americans (Twin Cities Habitat for Humanity, 2024) 17 . The program's success indicates that targeted interventions can effectively address the specific barriers that African American families face.

Credit Scoring and Financing Evolution offers additional opportunities to expand access. The Federal Housing Finance Agency's decision to allow VantageScore 4.0 alongside traditional FICO scores could significantly improve approval rates for Black applicants. VantageScore incorporates rent payment data and often produces higher scores for African American borrowers than traditional FICO models, potentially reducing the credit history barriers that account for 33.16% of Black mortgage denials.

Similarly, recent policies by Fannie Mae and Freddie Mac allowing rental payment history to count toward credit evaluation address one of the fundamental disadvantages faced by Black applicants. Since 33% of Black households have thin credit files compared to 18% of white households, alternative data sources can significantly expand the pool of mortgage-ready applicants.

The innovative approach of providing no-interest loans that are repaid only upon sale or refinancing removes traditional debt burden concerns while recycling program funds to serve additional families. This model addresses the primary barrier identified by most potential Black homebuyers: lack of funds for down payments and closing costs.

Down Payment Assistance Expansion represents another crucial opportunity for growth. Current programs demonstrate both significant demand and proven effectiveness. California's Building Black Wealth initiative has served over 9,000 families using $165 million in down payment assistance, while the GroundBreak Coalition's 2024 initiative aims to assist 1,000 new homeowners over three years and 11,000 families over a decade (GroundBreak Coalition, 2024)

Regional Market Opportunities emerge from demographic shifts and construction patterns. Markets in the South, where construction activity is highest and housing supply gaps are projected to close within three years, present particular opportunities for Black homeownership expansion. The concentration of African American populations in Southern markets aligns with regions showing the most promising supply and affordability trends.

Additionally, markets showing smaller denial rate gaps—such as Salt Lake City, San Antonio, and Fresno—indicate that local market conditions and lending practices can significantly influence access. Understanding and replicating the conditions that create more equitable lending practices could expand opportunities in additional markets.

Technology and Financial Innovation creates new tools for addressing traditional barriers. Online homebuyer education platforms, digital mortgage applications, and alternative verification methods can reduce some of the informational and procedural barriers that have historically limited access. Fannie Mae's HomeView education program, which has served nearly 50,000 homebuyers, demonstrates the potential for scalable, accessible education (Fannie Mae, 2025)

Community Partnership Models show significant promise for expanding reach and effectiveness. The success of programs that partner with churches, community organizations, and cultural institutions suggests that culturally competent, community-based approaches can achieve better outcomes than generic programs. These partnerships leverage existing trust relationships and cultural understanding to provide more effective support throughout the homebuying process.

The current landscape of African American homeownership presents a complex picture of persistent challenges alongside emerging opportunities. While mortgage denial rates remain 1.7 times higher for Black applicants and housing inventory constraints continue to create competitive disadvantages, demographic trends, policy innovations, and targeted program development create pathways for significant progress.

The convergence of 1.5 million Black households approaching prime homebuying age, the development of Special Purpose Credit Programs, the expansion of alternative credit scoring methods, and innovative down payment assistance models creates unprecedented potential for expanding Black homeownership. Success in capitalizing on these opportunities requires coordinated efforts that address both systemic barriers and individual preparation needs.

For organizations like The Power Is Now Media Inc., these trends underscore the importance of comprehensive approaches that combine education, advocacy, and direct assistance. The current moment presents both urgency—given the continuing disparities—and opportunity—given the aligned demographic and policy trends that could produce substantial progress in closing homeownership gaps.

BLACK ECONOMIC ALLIANCE

The pursuit of African American homeownership cannot be achieved in isolation from broader economic empowerment efforts. Organizations like the Black Economic Alliance demonstrate how coordinated action by business leaders can create systemic change that makes homeownership more attainable for African American families. Understanding their approach provides crucial context for our own homeownership initiative and illustrates how individual programs must connect to larger movements for economic justice.

The Black Economic Alliance stands as the nation's only coalition of Black business leaders and allies committed to driving economic equality for Black people (Black Economic Alliance, 2024) 67 . Founded in 2017 by politically engaged Black executives meeting in Bridgehampton, New York, the organization emerged from recognition that traditional advocacy approaches had not delivered sufficient economic progress for African American communities. By focusing specifically on work, wages, and wealth, the BEA leverages collective expertise, networks, and financial resources to dismantle persistent systems of racial inequality in pursuit of economic prosperity for Black Americans.

Recent developments showcase the organization's expanding influence and strategic approach.

The BEA Foundation's "Architecture For Action" initiative, unveiled in 2024, represents their comprehensive framework for driving Black economic prosperity (Black Economic Alliance Foundation, 2024) 68 . This framework recognizes that homeownership cannot be separated from broader economic empowerment—the same discriminatory practices that limit homeownership also constrain employment opportunities, business development, and wealth accumulation. Their research on Black Americans' perspectives on pathways to economic opportunity reveals that communities understand these interconnected challenges and seek comprehensive solutions rather than isolated interventions.

The organization's leadership includes individuals whose work directly impacts homeownership opportunities. Pamela Perry, vice president of equitable housing at Freddie Mac, leads initiatives supporting strategic efforts to expand access to homeownership in communities of color (Black Economic Alliance, 2024) 78 . Her role involves building a more equitable housing finance system by leading business strategy to help consumers establish credit, build generational wealth, and access housing opportunities. Perry's previous work in Freddie Mac's Legal division focused specifically on fair lending and access to credit for minority borrowers, demonstrating the type of institutional change necessary to address homeownership disparities.

The BEA's approach to political engagement offers lessons for homeownership advocates. Their 2024 voter mobilization program targeting infrequent Black voters in swing states including Georgia, Michigan, Nevada, North Carolina, and Pennsylvania demonstrates understanding that policy change requires political engagement. Housing policy, including down payment assistance programs, fair lending enforcement, and zoning reform, depends on elected officials who prioritize racial equity. The BEA's success in persuading hundreds of companies including Amazon, Bank of America, Microsoft, and Wells Fargo to support voting rights demonstrates how business pressure can influence policy outcomes.

Perhaps most relevant to homeownership efforts is the BEA's focus on wealth building rather than just income generation. John Hope Bryant's recognition in 2024 by TIME Magazine as one of "The Closers"—18 global leaders working to close the racial wealth gap—reflects understanding that sustainable economic progress requires wealth accumulation, not just higher wages (Black Economic Alliance, 2024) 78 . His book "Financial Literacy For All" addresses the knowledge gaps we identified as barriers to homeownership. Bryant's work with five U.S. Presidents demonstrates how financial empowerment connects to homeownership—families with better financial literacy and credit access can more successfully navigate the homeownership process.

The BEA's corporate engagement strategy provides a model for homeownership initiatives. Their work persuading major corporations to support racial equity initiatives demonstrates how business leadership can create policy change that benefits homeownership. For example, when financial services companies commit to fair lending practices or down payment assistance programs, they respond to organized business pressure as much as regulatory requirements. The BEA's Entrepreneurs Fund, anchored by Wells Fargo, shows how corporate partnerships can provide capital for wealth-building initiatives that complement homeownership programs.

The National Association of Real Estate Brokers

The National Association of Real Estate Brokers represents the oldest and most established organization specifically focused on promoting African American homeownership and "democracy in housing." Founded in 1947 in Tampa, Florida, NAREB emerged from the exclusion of African American real estate professionals from the National Association of Realtors and has spent over 75 years developing strategies to increase Black homeownership and wealth building through real estate (NAREB Convention, 2024).

NAREB's current activities demonstrate an evolved understanding of how to address homeownership disparities effectively. Their Building Black Wealth Tour, launched in 2024, conducted events in more than 100 cities nationwide with over 25,000 participants (NAREB Building Black Wealth Tour, 2025) 70 . This massive outreach effort targeted the more than two million mortgage-ready Black Americans with workshops on homeownership, property investment, and business development. The tour's partnerships with the Church of God In Christ, African American Mayors Association, National Bar Association, and major Black Greek organizations demonstrate the community-based approach necessary for sustained homeownership promotion.

The organization's strategic partnerships reveal sophisticated understanding of homeownership barriers. Major sponsors including Wells Fargo and Fannie Mae provide not just funding but also access to lending programs and mortgage products specifically designed for African American homebuyers. The HUD-approved NID Housing Counseling Agency's provision of free credit reports at events addresses the credit challenges we identified as homeownership barriers. These partnerships create comprehensive support that goes beyond education to provide actual pathways to homeownership.

NAREB's innovative programs address specific gaps in the real estate industry that limit African American homeownership. The NAREB Developers Academy represents a transformative initiative to increase diversity and representation in real estate development (NAREB Convention, 2024) 80 . By targeting areas with a shortage of Black developers, the academy addresses the supply-side challenges that limit affordable homeownership options in African American communities. Their goal of reaching over 500 participants by the end of 2025 demonstrates the scale necessary to create meaningful change in development patterns that have historically excluded African American communities.

This gender-focused approach acknowledges that successful homeownership promotion must address the specific challenges faced by African American women, including higher rates of single-headed households and different risk profiles than traditional lending assumes.

NAREB's 2025 initiatives demonstrate comprehensive understanding of contemporary homeownership challenges. Their Mid-Winter Conference theme "Navigating New Horizons" reflects recognition that traditional approaches to homeownership promotion require updating for current market conditions (Houston Style Magazine, 2025) 82 . The conference's focus on "transforming Black homeownership and wealth-building" acknowledges that homeownership must connect to broader wealth accumulation strategies to create lasting economic impact.

The organization's research and advocacy work provides crucial data for understanding homeownership trends. Their State of Housing in Black America (SHIBA) reports document the ongoing impacts of discriminatory policies and market conditions on African American homeownership. Their 2025 white papers on heir's properties and appraisal bias address specific contemporary challenges that traditional homeownership programs often overlook. Heir's property issues affect thousands of African American families who inherit property without clear title, while appraisal bias results in systematic undervaluation of homes in predominantly Black neighborhoods.

History's Weight: How Past Policies Still Shape Black Homeownership Today

The historical trajectory of African American homeownership reveals patterns that continue to shape contemporary housing disparities. From the post-Civil War Reconstruction era through the current moment, government policies, private market practices, and community responses have created the landscape we navigate today. Understanding this history illuminates why traditional approaches to promoting homeownership have achieved limited success and why targeted interventions like those pursued by the Black Economic Alliance and NAREB remain necessary

The complexity of current homeownership disparities becomes clearer when viewed through historical lens. The 27-28 percentage point gap between African American and white homeownership rates did not emerge from market forces alone, but from decades of intentional policy decisions that limited African American access to homeownership while subsidizing white wealth accumulation through housing. Contemporary data showing African Americans holding only 15.7% of white family wealth reflects not just individual economic differences, but the accumulated impact of historical exclusion from homeownership opportunities.

Recent trends suggest both the persistence of historical patterns and the potential for change through targeted intervention. The Urban Institute's analysis reveals that Black homeownership increased 2 percentage points between 2019 and 2021, from 42.2% to 44.2%, during a period of historically low interest rates (Urban Institute, 2025) 32 . However, these gains remain insufficient to recover losses from the Great Recession, let alone close the racial homeownership gap. The ongoing impact of historical discrimination means that even periods of economic growth and expanded credit access produce uneven benefits

The Housing Crisis of 2008–2010

The housing crisis of 2008-2010 represents a crucial inflection point that reversed decades of modest progress in African American homeownership and created disparities that persist today. Understanding the crisis's specific impact on African American communities provides essential context for current homeownership promotion efforts and illustrates why generic market-based solutions often fail to address racial disparities effectively.

The crisis hit African American families with devastating and disproportionate force. The National Community Reinvestment Coalition's analysis reveals that more than 240,000 African American homeowners lost their homes to foreclosure between 2005 and 2008 (National Community Reinvestment Coalition, 2021) 61 . About 8% of Black homeowners lost their homes to foreclosure from 2007 to 2009, compared to 4.5% of white homeowners at similar income levels—nearly twice the rate despite comparable financial circumstances (The Washington Post, 2019).

These disparities resulted not from African American families' financial irresponsibility, but from systematic targeting by predatory lenders. The crisis demonstrated how discriminatory lending practices operated through seemingly neutral market mechanisms. Subprime lenders specifically targeted African American and Latino communities for high-cost loans, often steering borrowers who qualified for prime loans into more expensive subprime products. Research shows that African American borrowers were charged 40-60 basis points higher APR and were 2% less likely to default compared to similar borrowers who were not steered into such loans, revealing the discriminatory nature of lending practices.

The geographic concentration of foreclosures in predominantly African American neighborhoods created cascading effects that extended far beyond individual families. Fairwood, Maryland—among the wealthiest Black neighborhoods in America—saw more than half of homeowners who bought there end up in foreclosure (The Washington Post, 2019) 85 . This pattern repeated nationwide, where entire communities that had represented African American wealth accumulation became symbols of economic devastation.

High-earning Black homeowners faced particular vulnerability during the crisis. Despite higher incomes that should have provided a financial cushion, they were 80% more likely to lose their homes than white counterparts with similar earnings (National Community Reinvestment Coalition, 2021) 84 . This counterintuitive finding reveals how discriminatory lending practices and limited wealth accumulation created fragility even among seemingly successful African American homeowners.

The crisis's timing proved particularly damaging because it struck just as African American homeownership was reaching historic highs. Black homeownership peaked at 49% between 2004-2006, representing decades of progress since the Fair Housing Act of 1968. The subsequent collapse erased these gains and pushed Black homeownership rates to levels not seen since the era of legal segregation. Current data shows Black homeownership hovering around 45%, still below pre-crisis peaks and substantially lower than the 49% rate achieved nearly two decades ago.

Recovery from the crisis has proved uneven and limited for African American families. While other racial groups have largely recovered their pre-crisis homeownership rates, African American homeownership continues to decline in many markets. The Urban Institute's analysis reveals that since 2001, the Black homeownership rate has seen the most dramatic drop of any racial or ethnic group, declining 5% compared with only 1% for white families (Urban Institute, 2018) 73 . The cohort most affected includes middle-aged homeowners ages 45-64 who, having lost homes during the crisis, find themselves unable to re-enter homeownership as they approach retirement age.

Credit standards tightened considerably following the crisis, creating additional barriers for potential African American homebuyers. Qualifying for mortgages became difficult for anyone with less than perfect credit, potentially blocking 6.3 million loans between 2009 and 2015 alone (Urban Institute, 2018) 86 . These stricter standards disproportionately affected African American families, who typically have lower average credit scores due to historical exclusion from credit markets and ongoing discrimination in credit reporting and scoring.

Negating Wealth-Building Opportunities for African Americans Post the Financial Crisis

The post-2008 recovery period created new forms of wealth inequality that continue to limit African American homeownership today.

While the crisis destroyed existing African American wealth through foreclosures, the recovery phase prevented many families from rebuilding wealth through homeownership, creating long-term disparities that extend beyond the crisis itself.

The most significant impact involved African Americans' exclusion from post-crisis homeownership opportunities. As home prices reached historic lows following the market collapse, families with available capital and credit access could purchase homes at substantial discounts. However, African American families, having lost wealth through foreclosures and job losses during the recession, typically lacked the resources to take advantage of these opportunities. Simultaneously, tightened lending standards meant that even creditworthy African American borrowers faced increased difficulty obtaining mortgage approval.

The National Association of Realtors' current data illustrates these ongoing disparities. White buyers represent 83% of total homebuyers, while Black buyers account for only 7%—significantly below African Americans' 13.6% share of the population (National Association of Realtors, 2025) 50 . This underrepresentation in the buyer market means African American families continue to miss wealth-building opportunities even as housing markets recover and appreciate.

Student loan debt has emerged as a particularly significant barrier to post-crisis homeownership for African American families. Current data shows that 42% of Black buyers report having student loan debt, compared to much lower rates for other racial groups (National Association of Realtors, 2025) 50 . African Americans with college degrees are five times more likely to default on student debt than white Americans, creating credit challenges that persist long after graduation and limit mortgage qualification.

The wealth implications extend beyond individual homeownership to affect entire communities and generations. The Federal Reserve's Survey of Consumer Finances shows Black families hold median wealth of $44,900, representing only 15.7% of white family wealth of $285,000 (Federal Reserve, 2023). Despite 61% wealth growth for Black families between 2019-2022, absolute dollar gaps actually widened by approximately $50,000, demonstrating how percentage gains can mask growing inequality in real terms.

Current African American homeowners face different financial profiles than their white counterparts, reflecting the ongoing impact of crisis-era losses and limited recovery opportunities. The average first home of an African American buyer is valued at $127,000 with average mortgage debt of $90,000, while white first-time buyers have average home values of $139,000 with only $75,000 in mortgage debt (National Community Reinvestment Coalition, 2021) 84 . This means African American families enter homeownership with higher debt-to-equity ratios, reducing their wealth-building potential and financial security.

Early Trends in African American Homeownership

Understanding the historical trajectory of African American homeownership reveals both the potential for rapid progress under supportive conditions and the devastating impact of discriminatory policies. The periods of greatest homeownership growth for African American families occurred during eras of intentional government support and economic expansion, while declines correspond to policy retrenchment and economic crisis.

The post-World War II era demonstrated the potential for dramatic homeownership expansion when government policy actively supported homeownership across racial lines. Between 1940 and 1960, African American homeownership rates rose dramatically by 15.2 percentage points, even during an era marked by systemic racism, Jim Crow laws, and legal housing discrimination (Population Reference Bureau, 2024) 74 . This increase occurred despite discriminatory FHA policies and redlining practices that limited African American access to government-backed mortgages.

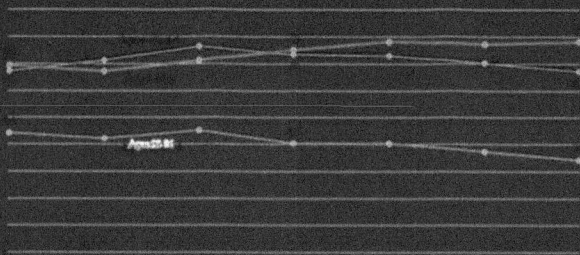

Figure 27. U.S. Homeownership Rate (%) by Age of Householder, 1960 to 2017. Source: Population Reference Bureau, 2020.

Several factors contributed to this remarkable growth despite discriminatory barriers. The post-WWII economic boom created employment opportunities and rising wages that enabled more African American families to save for homeownership. The lifting of wartime construction moratoriums increased housing supply, including in predominantly African American neighborhoods. Government issuance of low-interest mortgage rates, while often denied to African American families through discriminatory lending, still created market conditions that supported homeownership growth.

Importantly, this period's homeownership growth occurred through community-based strategies and alternative financing mechanisms when mainstream lending remained largely closed to African American families.

African American-owned banks, community savings organizations, and informal lending networks provided capital for homeownership when government programs excluded Black families. Real estate professionals like those who founded NAREB in 1947 created alternative market structures that served African American communities despite exclusion from white-dominated real estate organizations.

The Fair Housing Act of 1968 marked both progress and disappointment in African American homeownership trends. While the Act prohibited overt discrimination in housing transactions, it failed to produce the rapid homeownership increases that civil rights advocates anticipated. From 1960 to 1980, African American homeownership grew by only 6 percentage points, from 38% to 43.8%— a much slower rate than the previous two decades despite legal protections against discrimination.

This slower growth revealed the limitations of anti-discrimination legislation without accompanying affirmative measures to promote homeownership. Prohibiting discriminatory practices did not automatically create equal access to credit, down payment assistance, or homeownership education. The persistence of residential segregation meant that even non-discriminatory lending often resulted in unequal outcomes due to neighborhood-based lending patterns and property value disparities.

The 1990s brought renewed but modest homeownership growth for African American families. The decade began with Black homeownership at 44% and ended at 46.3%— small but consistent progress that continued through the early 2000s (National Community Reinvestment Coalition, 2021) 61 . This growth occurred during a period of economic expansion, increased availability of mortgage credit, and targeted government programs promoting homeownership among minority communities.

The peak of 49% African American homeownership between 2004-2006 represented the highest rates in American history and demonstrated the potential for dramatic progress under supportive market conditions. However, this peak also coincided with predatory lending practices that ultimately undermined sustainable homeownership. The fact that homeownership rates achieved their highest levels during a period of widespread lending abuse reveals both the potential for progress and the importance of ensuring that homeownership growth occurs through sustainable, wealth-building mechanisms rather than exploitative practices.

Closing the Gap Indefinitely!

Current trends and projections suggest that without dramatic intervention, the African American homeownership gap may persist indefinitely or even widen further. The Urban Institute's modeling indicates that reaching 60% Black homeownership by 2040—still 15 percentage points below current white homeownership rates—would require approximately 165,000 additional new Black homeowners annually over the next 20 years (National Community Reinvestment Coalition, 2021) 61 . This represents a massive increase over current production levels and would require coordinated intervention across multiple sectors and policy areas.

The mathematical challenge reveals the inadequacy of traditional approaches to homeownership promotion. Current homeownership programs typically serve hundreds or thousands of families annually, while closing the racial gap requires interventions that affect hundreds of thousands of families. The National Association of Realtors reports that Black buyers represent only 7% of all homebuyers despite comprising 13.6% of the population, illustrating the scale of change necessary to achieve proportional representation in homeownership markets.

Recent successful interventions provide models for the type of scaled response necessary to achieve meaningful progress. California's Building Black Wealth initiative served over 9,000 families using $165 million in down payment assistance, demonstrating the financial commitment required for significant impact. The GroundBreak Coalition's ambitious plan to provide down payment assistance for 11,000 families over a decade represents the type of systematic, sustained intervention necessary to achieve measurable progress.

Special Purpose Credit Programs emerging nationwide offer promising mechanisms for addressing homeownership disparities at scale. Twin Cities Habitat's Advancing Black Homeownership Program provides up to $50,000 for down payment assistance using flexible lending criteria specifically designed to address barriers facing African American homebuyers. These programs recognize that traditional underwriting standards often exclude creditworthy African American borrowers due to factors related to historical discrimination rather than actual lending risk.

The COVID-19 pandemic provided crucial evidence about the potential for rapid homeownership expansion under supportive market conditions. When mortgage interest rates fell to historic lows, African American homeownership increased 2 percentage points between 2019 and 2021—demonstrating that affordability improvements can quickly translate into homeownership gains. However, rising interest rates in 2022-2024 threaten to reverse these gains, illustrating how African American homeownership remains vulnerable to market conditions.

Technology and alternative data sources offer new possibilities for expanding credit access and homeownership qualification. Recognition of rental payment history, utility payments, and telecommunications bills in credit assessment could help address the credit challenges that limit African American mortgage approval rates

Automated underwriting systems that reduce human bias in loan approval decisions may help address discriminatory lending practices that persist despite fair lending regulations.

Policy changes at federal, state, and local levels remain essential for achieving sustained progress. These include expanded down payment assistance programs, stronger fair lending enforcement, zoning reforms that increase housing supply in high-opportunity neighborhoods, and tax policies that support homeownership among moderate-income families. The recent termination of federal fair housing enforcement funding demonstrates how policy retrenchment can quickly reverse progress, underscoring the importance of sustained political commitment to racial equity in housing.

Introduction to State of Ownership

Homeownership represents far more than a housing arrangement—it constitutes the foundation for economic stability, community development, and generational wealth building that shapes the trajectory of families and entire communities. The housing market and its intricate financing systems form critical components of a healthy economy, employing millions of people while generating substantial income for industry professionals and profits for investors. Yet despite the prominent place homeownership holds in American culture and political discourse as the cornerstone of the "American Dream," Black and other minority families continue to encounter formidable impediments to homeownership, most of which stem from the cumulative effects of poverty and systemic inequality that have operated across generations.

The contemporary landscape reveals both progress and persistent challenges. While homeownership options for Black Americans have shown improvement in certain periods following the 2008 financial crisis, the COVID-19 pandemic introduced new complexities that threatened the health, lives, and economic stability of Black families throughout the United States starting in early 2020. Understanding the current state of African American homeownership requires examining multiple interconnected factors that either facilitate or impede access to homeownership, from demographic trends to financial barriers to systemic discrimination that continues to operate despite decades of civil rights legislation.

The data tells a complex story of incremental progress shadowed by persistent disparities. Recent trends show modest gains in Black homeownership during certain periods, yet the fundamental gap between African American and white homeownership rates remains stubbornly wide. More concerning, the mechanisms that should promote homeownership—education, stable employment, financial literacy—often fail to produce equivalent outcomes for African American families compared to their white counterparts, suggesting that individual preparation alone cannot overcome structural barriers to homeownership access.

Current State of Ownership

Homeownership disparities continue to represent one of the most significant contributors to overall wealth inequality between racial groups in America. The most recent data from the U.S. Census Bureau reveals that as of 2023, the national homeownership rate stands at approximately 65.7%, reflecting a modest recovery from post-financial crisis lows but remaining below historical peaks (Eye on Housing, 2024) 35 . However, this aggregate figure masks dramatic disparities across racial and ethnic lines that persist despite decades of policy intervention and civil rights enforcement.

Between 2019 and 2022, non-white households experienced increases in homeownership rates that narrowed some previously existing disparities, yet substantial gaps remain. Current data shows that approximately 74.3% of white households own their homes, while only 45% of Black families and roughly half of Hispanic families achieve homeownership (Statista, 2024) 75 . This translates to a Black-white homeownership gap of approximately 29 percentage points—a disparity that has remained remarkably stable over recent decades despite various policy interventions designed to promote minority homeownership.

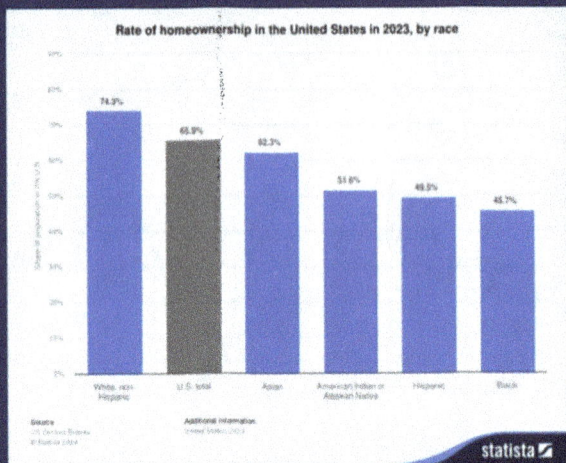

Figure 28. Rate of homeownership in the United States in 2023, by race. Source: Statista, 2025.

The persistence of these gaps becomes more troubling when viewed in historical context. The Fair Housing Act of 1968 prohibited overt discrimination in housing transactions, yet the current homeownership gap actually exceeds what existed when such discrimination was legal. This suggests that contemporary barriers to homeownership may be less visible than historical exclusions but equally effective in limiting African American access to homeownership opportunities.

Recent market conditions have created both opportunities and challenges for potential African American homebuyers.

The COVID-19 pandemic period saw historically low mortgage interest rates that enabled some families to achieve homeownership who might otherwise have been priced out of the market. The National Association of Realtors reports that Black homeownership increased modestly during this period, with Black buyers representing 7% of total homebuyers in 2024, though this remains significantly below their 13.6% share of the national population (National Association of Realtors, 2024).

However, the post-pandemic period has brought new challenges that threaten to reverse these modest gains. Rising interest rates, increasing home prices, and tightening credit standards have made homeownership less accessible for all groups, but particularly for African American families who typically have lower median incomes and less accumulated wealth to weather market volatility. The concentration of African American families in rental housing—where they face competition for affordable units and rising rental costs—creates additional pressure that makes saving for homeownership increasingly difficult.

Regional variations reveal how local market conditions and policy environments can either exacerbate or moderate national homeownership disparities. According to National Association of Realtors analysis, areas with the largest affordability gaps between white and Black households include Bridgeport, Connecticut; Charleston, South Carolina; Madison, Wisconsin; Minneapolis, Minnesota-Wisconsin; Portland, Maine; and San Francisco, California. In these markets, white households are twice as likely as Black households to afford homeownership (National Association of Realtors, 2024) 76 . San Francisco exemplifies extreme disparities, where white households have an affordability score of 0.75 compared to 0.35 for Black households, while Charleston shows white household affordability at 0.71 versus 0.34 for Black households.

Age, Gender, Education

AGE

Homeownership rates among younger Black families remain particularly concerning, reflecting broader generational challenges that may persist for decades. Recent demographic analysis reveals that homeownership disparities between Black and white individuals exist across all age categories, but the gaps are most pronounced among younger generations who represent the future of American homeownership.

Data from Redfin analysis demonstrates how these disparities compound across generations. Among millennials, only 33% of Black individuals own homes compared to 65% of white millennials—representing the largest homeownership gap of any generation and suggesting that traditional expectations about homeownership increasing with age may not hold for African American families (Population Reference Bureau, 2024) 74 . Even more troubling, Generation Z shows early signs of perpetuating these patterns, with white adults nearly twice as likely as Black adults to own homes. Specifically, 30% of white Generation Z adults achieve homeownership compared to only 16% of Black Generation Z adults.

These generational patterns reveal how contemporary barriers to homeownership may be intensifying rather than diminishing over time. Factors that previous generations could rely upon to support homeownership—stable employment, predictable career progression, affordable housing relative to income—have become less reliable for younger Americans generally, but particularly for young African Americans who face additional barriers related to student loan debt, employment discrimination, and limited access to family wealth for down payment assistance.

The persistence of homeownership gaps among older generations provides additional context for understanding these challenges. While racial disparities diminish somewhat among older Americans, they remain substantial across all age groups. Among Generation X, 52% of Black individuals own homes compared to 80% of white Generation X individuals. Baby Boomers show similar patterns, with 60% of Black Boomers owning homes compared to 85% of white Boomers. These patterns suggest that even with decades to accumulate resources and overcome barriers, African American families achieve homeownership at significantly lower rates than their white counterparts.

Age-related homeownership patterns also reflect the cumulative impact of historical discrimination and economic disadvantage. Older African Americans who achieved homeownership often did so during periods of legal segregation and limited financing options, suggesting remarkable persistence in pursuing homeownership despite systematic barriers. However, the wealth they accumulated through homeownership may be limited by factors such as property appreciation patterns in predominantly Black neighborhoods, refinancing experiences during predatory lending periods, and ongoing maintenance challenges related to limited resources for home improvements and repairs.

The implications for wealth building become particularly stark when considering how homeownership typically functions as the primary mechanism for middle-class wealth accumulation. Young African Americans who delay homeownership or never achieve it miss decades of potential equity building that could support retirement security, education funding for children, and intergenerational wealth transfer. This creates cycles where limited family wealth constrains homeownership opportunities for subsequent generations, perpetuating disparities across decades.

Age, Gender, Education

GENDER

Gender dynamics within African American homeownership reveal complex patterns that both reflect broader social trends and highlight specific challenges facing Black families. African Americans demonstrate a larger percentage of female-headed owner families than any other racial group, reflecting higher rates of single-parent households and the economic independence that homeownership can provide for women raising children alone. However, in comparison to other racial and ethnic groups, gender disparities in homeownership rates remain relatively minimal within the African American community.

This pattern reflects several intersecting factors that shape how African American women and men approach homeownership. Research consistently shows that African American women often serve as primary financial decision-makers in their households, including decisions about housing and homeownership. The higher education rates among African American women compared to men in their communities may provide additional resources and confidence for navigating the homeownership process, despite the financial challenges that student loan debt can create.

The prevalence of female-headed homeowner households in the African American community also reflects resilience in pursuing homeownership despite systemic barriers. Single-parent households typically face greater challenges in qualifying for mortgages due to single-income limitations and higher debt-to-income ratios. That African American women achieve homeownership at rates that maintain gender parity within their community suggests particular determination and strategic financial management, often achieved through extended family support networks and community-based assistance programs.

However, the relative gender parity in African American homeownership occurs within the context of overall lower homeownership rates for the community as a whole. While gender disparities may be minimal within the African American community, both African American men and women face substantially greater challenges achieving homeownership compared to their counterparts in other racial groups. This suggests that while gender may not create additional barriers within the African American community, racial barriers affect African American men and women relatively equally.

Contemporary data also reveals how gender intersects with other factors that influence homeownership outcomes. African American women are more likely to carry student loan debt and less likely to have access to family wealth for down payment assistance, yet they often demonstrate higher financial literacy and better credit management than their male counterparts. These competing factors create complex scenarios where individual financial strengths may be offset by structural barriers that affect the entire community.

EDUCATION

The relationship between education and homeownership reveals one of the most troubling aspects of contemporary housing inequality—how educational attainment that should facilitate homeownership often fails to produce expected outcomes for African American families. This disconnect between education and economic opportunity represents a fundamental challenge to traditional assumptions about pathways to middle-class stability and wealth building.

Current data reveals the stark reality that Black college graduates achieve homeownership rates only 3.2 percentage points higher than white high school dropouts.

Age, Gender, Education

EDUCATION

This counterintuitive finding demonstrates how educational achievement, while valuable, cannot by itself overcome the structural barriers that limit African American access to homeownership. White Americans without high school diplomas achieve homeownership at rates of approximately 60.5%, while Black Americans with four-year college degrees reach homeownership rates of only 56.4% (Urban Institute, 2019).

The primary mechanism through which education creates barriers rather than opportunities for African American homeownership involves student loan debt. An overwhelming 86.4% of Black college students carry student loan debt due to their disproportionate reliance on unsubsidized educational loans, compared to lower debt rates among white students who more often receive family financial support for education expenses. Recent data shows that Black home buyers report the highest share of student loan debt at 41%, with a median amount of $46,000 —representing a record high (National Association of Realtors, 2024)

The magnitude of student loan debt differences creates lasting disadvantages that persist long after graduation. Black and African American college graduates owe an average of $25,000 more in student loan debt than white college graduates. Four years after graduation, Black students owe an average of 188% more than white students initially borrowed, reflecting both higher initial debt loads and challenges with repayment that can result in negative amortization (Education Data, 2025) 78 . Black borrowers make average monthly payments of $258, compared to lower average payments for other racial groups, yet their balances often continue to grow due to interest accrual exceeding payment amounts.

The intersection of student loan debt with homeownership creates multiple barriers that compound over time. Higher debt payments reduce African American graduates' ability to save for down payments while also affecting their debt-to-income ratios that lenders use to evaluate mortgage applications. The Pew Research Center reports that 60% of still-indebted Black student loan borrowers do not have savings accounts, compared to lower rates among other racial groups, indicating how student loan payments can prevent the wealth accumulation necessary for homeownership (The Pew Charitable Trusts, 2024)

Paradoxically, survey research reveals that Black debt holders are less likely than their white and Hispanic counterparts to attribute student loans as a deterrent to homebuying. This finding suggests that despite facing objective financial constraints, Black student loan borrowers may perceive homeownership as such a distant aspiration that they do not immediately connect their debt burden to homeownership challenges. However, when asked about their intentions if freed from student loan debt, 28% of Black borrowers express intentions to invest in a home, compared to an average of 24% across all borrowers (National Association of Realtors, 2021)

The educational barrier to homeownership extends beyond individual debt burdens to reflect broader patterns of intergenerational wealth transfer that differ dramatically between racial groups. White households typically receive family financial support for education expenses and post-graduation wealth transfers that facilitate major purchases like homes. Black households, conversely, often transfer their increased post-college income to help extended family members, reducing their capacity to accumulate wealth for homeownership while supporting family networks that lack accumulated assets.

Earnings and Wealth

The earnings and wealth gap between African American and white families represents the foundational barrier underlying all other homeownership disparities. These economic differences reflect both contemporary discrimination and the accumulated effects of historical exclusions that prevented African American families from building wealth through homeownership and other investments across generations.

Current income data reveals persistent gaps that directly limit African American families' ability to afford homeownership. The median household income for white families reached $81,060 in 2022, compared to $52,860 for Black households—a difference of over $28,000 annually that compounds into substantial lifetime earnings differences. This income gap translates directly into reduced capacity to save for down payments, qualify for mortgages, and maintain homeownership costs including property taxes, insurance, and maintenance.

However, income differences represent only part of the economic challenge facing African American families seeking homeownership.

Wealth disparities are far more dramatic and consequential for homeownership access. The median net worth of white households was $250,400 in 2022, more than ten times higher than the median net worth of Black households at $24,520. This wealth gap means that even African American families with middle-class incomes typically lack the accumulated assets necessary for homeownership transitions and ongoing ownership stability.

The composition of African American wealth reveals both the importance of homeownership for the community and the limited diversification of assets available to most families. Home equity comprises 67% of Black households' median net worth, compared to 58% for white households, despite white families having substantially higher homeownership rates and higher median homeowner equity. This concentration of wealth in homeownership makes African American families particularly vulnerable to housing market fluctuations while also limiting their access to liquid assets that could support major purchases or economic emergencies

The total assets comparison reveals the full scope of economic disadvantage. The typical white household holds total assets of $808,000—an amount twice that of the typical Black household. This difference affects homeownership in multiple ways, from the obvious impact on down payment capacity to the less visible effects on mortgage qualification, interest rates, and ongoing financial security that enables families to maintain homeownership through economic challenges.

Recent analysis highlighting extreme wealth concentration provides additional context for understanding these disparities. The collective wealth of the 400 richest Americans equals the combined wealth of 48 million Black Americans, illustrating how wealth concentration at the top of the economic distribution intersects with racial wealth gaps to create particularly challenging conditions for African American wealth building (Federal Reserve, 2023) 7

Regional and local variations in the earnings and wealth gap create geographic patterns that significantly affect homeownership opportunities. Asian Americans demonstrate the highest median income levels nationwide, with nearly 50% earning more than $100,000 annually, which translates into greater housing affordability and homeownership access.

Geographic Location

Geographic variations in homeownership affordability and access reveal how local market conditions, policy environments, and historical development patterns combine to create dramatically different opportunities for African American families across different regions and metropolitan areas. These location-based differences suggest that homeownership disparities are not uniform national phenomena but rather reflect the interaction of national trends with local factors that can either exacerbate or moderate barriers to African American homeownership.

Metropolitan areas with the largest affordability disparities between white and Black households demonstrate how local housing costs, income patterns, and historical development create particularly challenging conditions for African American homeownership. The National Association of Realtors identifies Bridgeport, Connecticut; Charleston, South Carolina; Madison, Wisconsin; Minneapolis, Minnesota-Wisconsin; Portland, Maine; and San Francisco, California as areas where white households are twice as likely as Black households to afford homeownership.

San Francisco exemplifies extreme geographic disparities, where white households achieve an affordability score of 0.75 while Black households score only 0.35. This gap reflects not only the region's extraordinarily high housing costs but also employment patterns, historical exclusion from high-paying technology sector jobs, and limited access to equity from previous homeownership that could support upgrading to more expensive markets. Charleston, South Carolina shows similar patterns with white household affordability at 0.71 compared to Black household affordability at 0.34, despite lower absolute housing costs than San Francisco.

Urban versus rural patterns also create different homeownership opportunities and challenges for African American families. Rural areas typically demonstrate higher overall homeownership rates, reaching 81% compared to 60% in urban areas nationally. However, rural African American homeownership often occurs in areas with limited economic opportunities, lower property appreciation rates, and reduced access to credit and professional services that could support homeownership transitions and maintenance. Urban areas offer greater economic opportunities and more diverse housing options but also present higher costs and more competitive housing markets that can exclude families with limited resources.

State-level variations reveal how policy environments and regional economic conditions create different contexts for African American homeownership. States with higher concentrations of Black borrowers, such as Montana, Michigan, and Mississippi at 6% each, show different patterns in terms of interest rates and lending conditions. Montana presents particularly challenging conditions, with nearly one in three Black borrowers receiving mortgage rates higher than 6%. Mississippi, despite having 25% of Black borrowers facing rates above 6%, represents one of the states with the highest percentages of Black borrowers among all states, suggesting both opportunities and challenges in different geographic contexts.

Regional economic development patterns also influence how effectively African American families can leverage homeownership for wealth building. Areas with strong property appreciation, diverse economic opportunities, and growing populations offer greater potential for homeownership to generate wealth over time. Conversely, regions with declining populations, limited economic diversity, or environmental challenges may offer more affordable homeownership options but less wealth-building potential over the long term.

Opportunities in the Market

Current market dynamics reveal both the persistence of underrepresentation and emerging opportunities that could support expanded African American homeownership. The demographic composition of homebuyers demonstrates continuing disparities, with white homebuyers dominating at 81% of the market while African American buyers represent only 7%—significantly below their 13.6% population share. Asian and Pacific Islander buyers, along with other groups, each represent 6% of the market, indicating how multiple minority communities remain underrepresented in homeownership markets.

However, within these overall patterns, specific trends suggest potential pathways for increasing African American homeownership participation. The 2023 Profile of Home Buyers and Sellers reveals that 24% of African American home purchasers choose multigenerational housing, compared to only 12% of white buyers. This preference reflects practical strategies for managing homeownership costs while providing care for elderly relatives and maintaining family connections. Multigenerational housing can enable homeownership by allowing families to pool resources, share expenses, and provide mutual support that makes homeownership more financially sustainable.

The motivations driving different racial groups toward homeownership reveal important insights about market opportunities and barriers. Research shows that 43% of Black buyers, 42% of Pacific Islander buyers, and 40% of Hispanic/Latino buyers are driven primarily by the dream of owning their own home, compared to only 23% of white/Caucasian buyers. This higher level of aspiration among minority communities suggests substantial latent demand for homeownership that could be activated through appropriate programs and policies.

However, other motivational patterns reveal how different starting points create different homeownership challenges. Only 9% of Black purchasers are motivated by the need for a larger home, compared to 13% of Asian buyers, 12% of Hispanic buyers, and 10% of white buyers. This difference likely reflects how many African American families are pursuing homeownership for the first time rather than upgrading from previous homeownership, indicating different support needs and different potential program interventions.

Real estate professional utilization patterns suggest both opportunities and challenges in market access. Current data shows that 86% of Black homebuyers and 89% of white purchasers use real estate agents or brokers, indicating similar recognition of professional assistance needs. However, the effectiveness of these professional relationships may vary significantly based on agent knowledge about programs specifically available to minority homebuyers, cultural competency, and networks within African American communities.

The concentration of African American buyers among first-time purchasers presents both opportunities and challenges for market expansion. National Association of Realtors data indicates that 49% of Black buyers are first-time purchasers, compared to 43% of Asian buyers, 41% of Hispanic buyers, and only 20% of white buyers. This concentration among first-time buyers suggests that programs specifically designed for first-time purchasers could have disproportionate benefits for African American homeownership, but it also indicates that Black buyers lack the advantages that come from previous homeownership experience, existing equity, and established relationships with real estate professionals.

State of the Black Borrower Mortgage Market

The mortgage lending landscape for African American borrowers in 2024-2025 reveals persistent disparities that extend beyond simple approval or denial decisions to encompass every aspect of the lending process. From interest rates and loan terms to application processing and post-closing outcomes, Black borrowers continue to face systematically different treatment that compounds over time to create substantial wealth implications. Understanding these disparities requires examining not just the numbers, but the mechanisms through which seemingly neutral lending practices produce racially disparate outcomes.

Recent comprehensive analysis of the mortgage market reveals both troubling continuities and concerning new developments in lending disparities. The National Community Reinvestment Coalition's 2025 analysis of Consumer Financial Protection Bureau data covering 2024 lending activity shows that while lending to Hispanic and Asian borrowers increased their market share, Black lending actually declined (National Community Reinvestment Coalition, 2025) 81 . This finding proves particularly significant given that housing represents the primary vehicle for wealth building in America, and the gap between Black and white homeownership rates remains the biggest factor driving vast wealth disparities between racial groups.

The complexity of contemporary lending disparities becomes clear when examining how seemingly race-neutral underwriting criteria systematically produce unequal outcomes. While overt discrimination based on race has been illegal for decades, sophisticated analysis reveals how factors like credit scoring, debt-to-income calculations, and property appraisal practices create barriers that disproportionately affect African American borrowers. These mechanisms often operate below the threshold of legal challenge while producing discriminatory results that perpetuate historical patterns of exclusion.

Home Purchase Loans by Race

Shown as a percent of loans where the borrower indicate a race or ethnicity.

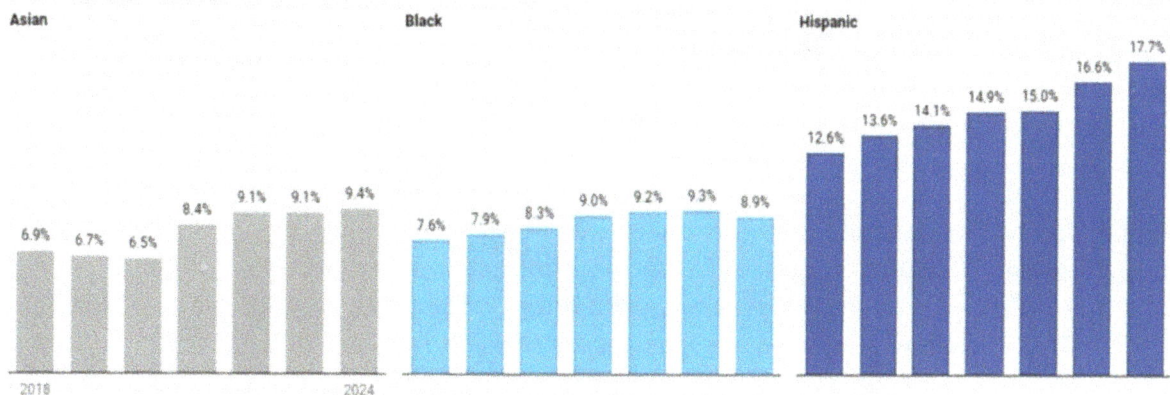

Figure 29. Home Purchase Loans by Race. Source: National Community Reinvestment Coalition, 2025.

Rates of Interest

Interest rate disparities represent one of the most direct and measurable forms of lending discrimination affecting African American borrowers today. Unlike approval decisions that may be explained by multiple factors, interest rate differences for similarly qualified borrowers reveal the ongoing impact of discriminatory practices in contemporary lending markets. Current research demonstrates that these disparities persist across income levels, geographic markets, and lending institutions, suggesting systematic rather than isolated instances of bias.

The Joint Center for Housing Studies' groundbreaking analysis using 2019 American Housing Survey data revealed patterns that challenge conventional explanations for interest rate disparities. Black homeowners with household incomes between $75,000-$100,000 received higher interest rates than white homeowners earning $30,000 or less—a disparity that cannot be explained by creditworthiness or income alone (Joint Center for Housing Studies, 2024) 82 . This finding demonstrates how discrimination operates independently of borrowers' actual financial qualifications, with high-income Black borrowers receiving worse terms than low-income white borrowers.

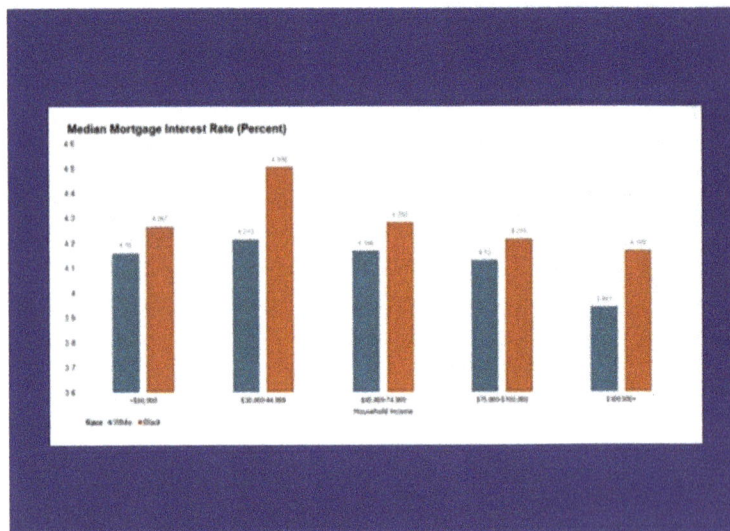

Figure 30. High-Income Black Homeowners Have Higher Interest Rates than Low-Income White Homeowners. Source: Joint Center for Housing Studies, 2021

Local market analysis provides even more stark evidence of discriminatory lending practices. A 2024 study of three major banks in New York City—Bank of America, Citibank, and Chase—found that Black homeowners consistently received higher interest rates than white borrowers with similar financial profiles (THE CITY, 2024) 83 . White borrowers earning less than $100,000 received average interest rates of approximately 3.93%, compared to 4.20% for Black borrowers earning more than $100,000. This analysis controlled for income and debt levels while finding that credit scores were not available in the data, suggesting that even unknown credit differences could not explain the full magnitude of the disparities observed.

The persistence of interest rate disparities despite regulatory oversight reflects the sophistication of contemporary discriminatory practices. University of California at Berkeley researchers analyzing nearly 7 million 30-year mortgages found that Black and Latino applicants were charged an average of nearly 0.08% higher interest rates compared to white borrowers in face-to-face transactions (CBS News, 2019) 84 . While this percentage may appear small, it translates to hundreds of millions of dollars extracted from minority homeowners annually. The study found that both face-to-face and online lenders rejected 1.3 million creditworthy Black and Latino applicants between 2008 and 2015 —applicants who researchers determined "would have been accepted had the applicant not been in these minority groups."

Technology-mediated lending offers some promise for reducing discriminatory outcomes while revealing the extent of human bias in traditional lending processes. The Berkeley study found that app-based mortgage approvals were 40% less likely to result in higher mortgage rates for borrowers of color, suggesting that removing human discretion from parts of the lending process can improve outcomes (CBS News, 2019) 99 . However, even online and app-based lenders continued to charge minority borrowers higher rates, though terms were slightly better than face-to-face transactions, indicating that algorithmic bias can reproduce human discrimination patterns.

Geographic patterns in interest rate disparities reveal how local market conditions intersect with racial bias to create varying levels of discrimination across different regions. Financial Samurai's analysis indicates that mortgage rates differ significantly by race nationwide, with Asian borrowers typically receiving the lowest rates and Black borrowers facing the highest rates (Financial Samurai, 2025) 85 . These patterns suggest that discrimination operates not just through individual lender bias but through broader market mechanisms that consistently disadvantage African American borrowers regardless of their specific qualifications or the particular institutions they approach for financing.

Refinancing disparities compound the impact of higher initial interest rates by preventing African American borrowers from accessing lower rates when market conditions improve. The Joint Center for Housing Studies found that only 20% of Black homeowners have previously refinanced their mortgages, compared to 31% of white homeowners (Joint Center for Housing Studies, 2024) 97 . Even when Black homeowners do refinance, they achieve smaller interest rate reductions—a median decrease of 22 basis points from 4.319% to 4.093%—while still maintaining rates 20 basis points higher than white homeowners who refinanced.

Denials of Mortgage Loans

Mortgage denial patterns reveal the most direct form of lending discrimination, where qualified African American applicants are systematically excluded from homeownership opportunities that would be available to similarly situated white applicants. Current data demonstrates that these disparities have persisted and in some cases worsened despite decades of fair lending regulations and enforcement efforts. Understanding denial patterns requires examining not just outright rejections but also the various forms of "soft denials" that prevent potential borrowers from completing the application process.

The Urban Institute's comprehensive analysis of Home Mortgage Disclosure Act data reveals the scope of contemporary denial disparities. Black borrowers faced denial rates of 27.1% compared to 13.6% for white borrowers in recent lending cycles (Urban Institute, 2025) 86 . This represents a denial rate exactly twice as high for Black applicants, indicating systematic rather than incidental discrimination. These disparities become even more concerning when examining specific loan types and purposes, where denial rates reveal barriers to both initial homeownership and wealth building through refinancing and equity extraction.

Application withdrawal patterns suggest that official denial rates may understate the full impact of discriminatory lending practices. Asian (16.2%) and Black (15.0%) applicants are more likely to withdraw mortgage applications before receiving formal denials, while Hispanic (3.6%) and Black (3.8%) applicants are more likely to have files closed for incompleteness (Urban Institute, 2025) 100 . These "soft denials" may represent cases where discriminatory treatment during the application process discourages borrowers from continuing, or where lenders apply different standards for application completeness based on applicant race.

Federal Reserve research provides compelling evidence that denial disparities cannot be explained by legitimate underwriting factors. The Minneapolis Federal Reserve's analysis of confidential HMDA data with full credit scores found that lender-reported denial reasons do not explain racial disparities in approval rates (Federal Reserve Bank of Minneapolis, 2024) 11 . Even when controlling for credit history and financial qualifications, Black applicants remained significantly more likely to be denied for credit history reasons or to receive "Other" as a denial explanation—a category that provides no transparency about actual decision-making factors.

Refinancing denials reveal additional layers of discrimination that affect existing homeowners' ability to build wealth and manage housing costs. The New York City analysis found that the three major banks denied Black homeowners refinancing applications almost twice as often as white homeowners, with nearly 25% of Black applicants rejected compared to just under 13% of white applicants (THE CITY, 2024) 98 . These disparities prevent Black homeowners from accessing the equity they have built in their homes and from reducing their housing costs when interest rates decline.

Cash-out refinancing denials pose particular barriers to wealth building for African American homeowners who may need to access home equity for business investments, education expenses, or other wealth-building opportunities. The Urban Institute found high denial rates for cash-out refinances, particularly for Black and Hispanic households, suggesting that even homeowners with sufficient equity from recent price appreciation face barriers to extracting cash from their housing wealth (Urban Institute, 2025) 101 . This pattern limits the ability of Black homeowners to leverage their housing investment for broader wealth building purposes.

The concentration of denials among specific lender types reveals how market segmentation can perpetuate discriminatory outcomes. Black families rely on Federal Housing Administration lending for 45% of their purchase loans, making them particularly vulnerable to changes in FHA lending standards and practices (Urban Institute, 2018) 86 . When credit standards tighten or FHA loan limits fail to keep pace with housing costs, Black borrowers face disproportionate impacts because they have fewer alternative lending sources than white borrowers with greater wealth and credit access.

Income

Income disparities between African American and white households provide the foundation for many of the lending differences observed in contemporary mortgage markets, while also revealing how historical discrimination continues to limit wealth accumulation opportunities across generations. Understanding current income patterns requires recognizing both the persistence of wage gaps and the ways that income differences interact with lending practices to create compounding disadvantages for African American borrowers.

Current income data demonstrates the continuation of historical wage disparities concerning new developments in the post-pandemic economy. The National Association of Realtors' analysis reveals that only 20% of Black Americans earn more than $100,000 annually, compared to 35% of white Americans, 25% of Hispanic Americans, and nearly 50% of Asian Americans (National Association of Realtors, 2025) 50 . This concentration of Asian Americans in higher income brackets helps explain their advantageous position in mortgage markets, while the concentration of Black Americans in lower income brackets creates systematic barriers to homeownership qualification.

The Federal Reserve's Survey of Consumer Finances provides additional context for understanding how income differences translate into homeownership barriers. Black families hold median wealth of $44,900, representing only 15.7% of white family wealth of $285,000 (Federal Reserve, 2023) 3 . This wealth disparity proves more significant than income differences alone because homeownership requires not just sufficient income to make mortgage payments, but also accumulated wealth to cover down payments, closing costs, moving expenses, and the unexpected repairs that homeownership entails.

Recent economic trends have created mixed outcomes for income growth across racial groups. Between 2017 and 2019, wages increased 8% across all racial groups, but between 2020 and 2022 growth slowed to only 3% across all races (National Association of Realtors, 2025) 50 . This deceleration in wage growth occurred during a period of rising housing costs, creating affordability challenges that disproportionately affected lower-income workers who are disproportionately African American.

The interaction between income levels and lending practices creates additional barriers for African American borrowers beyond what income differences alone would predict. Even high-income Black borrowers face lending challenges that their white counterparts do not experience. The Joint Center for Housing Studies research showing that high-income Black borrowers receive worse interest rates than low-income white borrowers illustrates how income alone cannot protect African American borrowers from discriminatory treatment.

Student loan debt represents a particularly significant factor affecting the relationship between income and homeownership qualification for African American families.

Current data shows that 42% of Black buyers report having student loan debt, compared to lower rates for other racial groups (National Association of Realtors, 2025) 50 . Black college graduates owe an average of $52,726 in student loan debt—$25,000 more than white college graduates (Education Data, 2025) 93 . Four years after graduation, Black students owe an average of 188% more than white students initially borrowed, creating long-term barriers to wealth accumulation and mortgage qualification.

Loan Amount

The relationship between loan amounts and borrower race reveals how wealth disparities and lending practices interact to create different homebuying experiences across racial groups. African American borrowers consistently require larger loan amounts relative to their incomes and home values, reflecting both their lower average wealth and the systematically higher costs they face in housing markets. These patterns create long-term wealth implications that extend far beyond the initial mortgage transaction.

Student loan debt represents the most significant factor affecting loan amounts for African American homebuyers, creating debt-to-income ratio challenges that limit mortgage qualification and purchasing power. Black college graduates carry federal student loan debt averaging $53,430, compared to $51,810 for white borrowers—a difference that compounds over time due to different repayment patterns and default rates (Education Data, 2025) 93 . Black borrowers owe $7,400 more on average than white borrowers at graduation, with the gap widening to $25,000 more over the four years following graduation.

The concentration of student loan debt among African American borrowers creates particular challenges for mortgage underwriting.

Education Data analysis reveals that 41% of African American homebuyers carry student loan debt—the highest rate among all racial groups (Education Data, 2025) 93 . Federal Reserve research indicates that a $1,000 increase in student loan debt lowers the homeownership rate by approximately 1.8% for public four-year college graduates, translating to an average delay of about four months in achieving homeownership (Housing Matters, 2022).

The persistence of student loan debt among Black borrowers reflects broader patterns of wealth inequality that affect both educational financing and homeownership prospects. Over 50% of Black student borrowers report their net worth is less than their outstanding student loan debt, compared to 52% of Asian and white borrowers who have net worth exceeding their student loan obligations (Education Data, 2025) 93 . This negative net worth position creates particular challenges for homeownership because it limits the ability to accumulate down payment savings while managing existing debt obligations.

Default patterns on student loans create additional barriers to mortgage qualification that disproportionately affect African American borrowers.

Black college graduates are five times more likely to default on student loans than white graduates, creating credit challenges that persist long after graduation and directly impact mortgage eligibility (Urban Institute, 2022) 88 . These defaults typically occur despite borrowers having sufficient education credentials for higher-income employment, suggesting that the defaults reflect broader economic disadvantages rather than educational inadequacy.

Geographic factors compound the impact of higher loan amounts for African American borrowers by concentrating them in markets where homes cost more relative to local incomes. The National Community Reinvestment Coalition's analysis shows that Black borrowers often face higher housing costs in the markets where they are able to purchase homes, requiring larger loans relative to their incomes even when purchasing modestly priced properties (National Community Reinvestment Coalition, 2021).

LTV Ratios and Down Payments

Loan-to-value ratios and down payment patterns reveal how wealth disparities translate directly into different lending terms and long-term financial outcomes for African American homebuyers. These differences reflect not just current economic circumstances but the accumulated impact of generations of wealth-building exclusion that leaves Black families with fewer resources for homeownership despite having comparable incomes to white families.

Current data demonstrates stark differences in down payment capacity across racial groups. The National Association of Realtors reports that typical down payments are highest among Asian buyers at 21% and white buyers at 19%, while Black and Hispanic buyers typically make smaller down payments despite similar income levels (National Association of Realtors, 2025) 50 . These differences reflect wealth disparities rather than income differences, as Black buyers often earn sufficient income to support mortgage payments but lack accumulated wealth for substantial down payments.

Loan-to-value ratio patterns illustrate the long-term implications of wealth disparities for homeownership sustainability and wealth building. 44.4% of African American households have LTV ratios exceeding 90% at loan origination, compared to only 29.7% of white households (National Association of Realtors, 2025) 50 . Higher LTV ratios indicate both greater lending risk and reduced wealth-building potential, as borrowers with minimal equity have less financial cushion to weather economic shocks and receive smaller returns from housing appreciation.

The sources of down payment funds reveal additional aspects of wealth inequality that affect African American homebuyers. Black buyers use 401(k)/pension funds (11%) and community/government down payment assistance programs (5%) more than any other racial group (National Association of Realtors, 2025. While these resources provide valuable support for homeownership access, relying on retirement funds for down payments can undermine long-term wealth building by reducing resources available for retirement security.

Conversely, Black and Latino borrowers are significantly less likely to receive down payment assistance from family members or to use proceeds from previous property sales—sources that typically provide larger amounts and don't require borrowers to deplete other wealth-building accounts (National Association of Realtors, 2025) 50 . This pattern reflects the intergenerational nature of wealth disparities, where African American families cannot draw on family wealth accumulated through previous generations' homeownership because that wealth accumulation was prevented by discriminatory policies.

The Federal Reserve's research reveals the broader implications of high LTV lending for African American wealth building. Nearly 20% of Black families have zero or negative net worth, compared to just 9% of white families (Federal Reserve, 2023) 3 . This lack of financial cushion makes it difficult to weather economic shocks and maintain good credit, creating vulnerabilities that persist throughout the homeownership experience and can lead to foreclosure during economic downturns.

Private mortgage insurance requirements and costs disproportionately affect African American borrowers due to their higher LTV ratios, adding to housing costs and reducing the wealth-building potential of homeownership. Borrowers with LTV ratios above 80% typically must purchase private mortgage insurance, creating additional monthly costs that reduce available income for other wealth-building activities and make homeownership more expensive relative to renting.

The comprehensive analysis of current lending disparities reveals a mortgage market where African American borrowers face systematically different treatment across every aspect of the lending process. From higher interest rates and denial rates to larger loan amounts and higher LTV ratios, Black borrowers encounter barriers that compound over time to create substantial wealth implications extending far beyond individual mortgage transactions.

The 2024-2025 data demonstrates concerning persistence and in some cases worsening of lending disparities despite decades of fair lending regulation and enforcement. Black borrowers continue to receive higher interest rates than white borrowers with lower incomes, face denial rates twice as high as white applicants, and require larger loans with higher LTV ratios due to wealth constraints. These patterns suggest that current regulatory approaches and market mechanisms have proved insufficient to address the structural factors that create discriminatory lending outcomes.

The interconnected nature of these disparities reveals why isolated interventions typically fail to achieve meaningful progress. Student loan debt affects income available for mortgage payments, which influences loan amounts and LTV ratios, which affect interest rates and approval decisions, which determine long-term wealth building potential. Breaking this cycle requires coordinated interventions that address multiple barriers simultaneously rather than treating individual symptoms of systematic discrimination.

Contemporary lending discrimination operates primarily through seemingly neutral criteria that systematically disadvantage African American borrowers rather than through overt racial bias. Credit scoring systems that don't account for rental payment history, debt-to-income calculations that penalize student loan debt, and appraisal practices that undervalue homes in predominantly Black neighborhoods create barriers that appear race-neutral while producing racially disparate outcomes.

The evidence strongly supports expanding alternative underwriting approaches that can more accurately assess African American borrowers' creditworthiness and homeownership potential. Special Purpose Credit Programs, recognition of rental payment histo-ty, flexible treatment of student loan debt, and expanded down payment assistance represent promising approaches for addressing current disparities. However, achieving meaningful progress will require sustained commitment from government, private sector, and community organizations working together to address the systematic nature of contemporary lending discrimination.

The mortgage lending disparities documented here represent more than individual inconveniences or higher costs—they constitute a systematic mechanism through which wealth inequality perpetuates across generations. Each Black homebuyer who receives a higher interest rate, faces an unjustified denial, or must accept higher LTV ratios experiences not just immediate financial harm but reduced wealth-building potential that affects their family's economic prospects for decades. Addressing these disparities therefore represents both a matter of individual fairness and a crucial component of broader efforts to achieve racial equity in wealth accumulation and economic opportunity.

Where We Will Start

The Power Is Now Media Inc. is based in Riverside, California, positioning us at the epicenter of one of America's most complex and troubling homeownership stories. When we examine where to begin our African American Homeownership Initiative, California provides both the most urgent need and the most instructive example of how historical discrimination creates persistent contemporary barriers. California's Black homeownership rate today stands at approximately 38-41% compared to nearly 70% for white families—a gap that is not only wider than the national average but represents a rate lower now than it was in the 1960s when it was completely legal to discriminate against Black homebuyers (California Housing Finance Agency, 2024

This stark reality demands our immediate attention and action. The latest data from 2024-2025 reveals that California's housing discrimination persists in forms both overt and subtle, with the California Civil Rights Department conducting over 120 phone tests and nearly 100 in-person tests across Los Angeles County and Ventura County in 2024 alone (California Civil Rights Department, 2025)[2]. The results paint a disturbing picture: 54% of tested properties demonstrated discrimination based on source of income, 22% showed racial discrimination against Black applicants, 26% discriminated against families with children, and 23% discriminated based on disability (California Civil Rights Department, 2025).

Understanding why California's African American homeownership rate remains so devastatingly low requires examining how the state's history of systematic exclusion continues to reverberate through contemporary housing markets. California's history of housing discrimination against African Americans represents one of the most comprehensive and deliberate exclusion campaigns in American history, beginning with the state's first governor and continuing through sophisticated modern practices that maintain racial segregation while appearing race-neutral.

California's Historical Foundation of Exclusion

The roots of California's current homeownership crisis trace directly to the state's founding philosophy and early political leadership. When Peter Hardeman Burnett became California's first governor in 1849, he brought with him an explicit vision of creating a whites-only American West. This was not a subtle preference or an unspoken assumption—it was an openly declared political platform that shaped California's early institutions and policies in ways that continue to limit African American homeownership today.

Burnett's background provides crucial context for understanding how deliberate California's exclusion policies were. As a former slaveholder from Tennessee who had actively promoted Oregon's Black exclusionary laws, Burnett represented the systematic transplantation of Southern racial policies to Western territories. His infamous "Lash Law" in Oregon, which allowed for the physical punishment of African Americans who refused to leave the state, demonstrated the lengths to which he would go to maintain white supremacy (Oregon Historical Society, 2019).

The story of Sandy Jones, Robert, and Carter Perkins illustrates how quickly these exclusionary policies translated into action in California. These three former slaves from Mississippi arrived in Ophir, California, in 1851 during the gold rush, believing they had found the freedom and opportunity that California promised. Within months, they had built a successful freight business and accumulated over $3,000 each in personal property—substantial wealth for any American at that time (Bancroft Library, University of California Berkeley, 1885.

Their success, however, made them targets. In April 1852

armed white men invaded their cabin at night, bound them, and transported them to Sacramento using their own wagon and mule team. The Sacramento judge pronounced them fugitive slaves and ordered their return to Mississippi, despite California's status as a free state (California State Archives, 1852) 92 . This dramatic reversal of fortune occurred just six weeks after California passed its Fugitive Slave Law, which retroactively denied freedom to any enslaved person who had entered California as a territory, even though they had been legally free under territorial law.

This incident reveals the deliberate nature of California's exclusionary policies. The Fugitive Slave Law was not a response to federal pressure or constitutional requirement—it was a calculated effort to remove successful African Americans from the state and send a message to others who might consider California as a destination for building wealth and establishing communities.

The Persistence of Exclusion Through Legal Mechanisms

California's exclusion of African Americans evolved through increasingly sophisticated legal mechanisms that maintained the effect of racial barriers while adapting to changing constitutional requirements. The progression from overt exclusion attempts to subtle but effective discrimination demonstrates how systematic racial barriers adapt to legal challenges while maintaining their fundamental purpose. During the 1849 Constitutional Convention, the depth of anti-Black sentiment became clear when Morton M. McCarver, a delegate from Kentucky, introduced a resolution declaring Black people "insolent and defiant, and if in sufficient numbers, would become dangerous" (Proceedings of the California Constitutional Convention, 1849) 93 . While this specific resolution failed, the sentiment it represented influenced California policy for generations.

The failure of overt exclusion laws led to more subtle but equally effective forms of discrimination. When direct prohibition proved impossible, California legislators and local officials developed what would become a template for maintaining racial segregation through seemingly neutral policies. Mining regulations excluded African Americans from the most profitable claims. Residential restrictions concentrated Black families in specific neighborhoods. Employment limitations prevented African Americans from competing in lucrative professions.

These early patterns established precedents for the sophisticated discrimination that would emerge in the twentieth century. By the time federal fair housing laws prohibited overt racial discrimination, California had developed complex systems of exclusion that operated through seemingly neutral mechanisms like credit requirements, neighborhood character preservation, and property value protection.

The Evolution to Modern Housing Discrimination

The civil rights era brought legal prohibitions against overt housing discrimination, but California's response demonstrates how deeply embedded exclusionary practices adapted rather than disappeared. The passage of the California Fair Housing Act of 1963, known as the Rumford Act, represented a high point of civil rights progress, prohibiting discrimination in public housing and private residential properties with more than five units (California State Archives, 1963).

The immediate backlash against the Rumford Act reveals the persistence of exclusionary sentiment among white Californians. The California Real Estate Association led a campaign that successfully placed Proposition 14 on the 1964 ballot, which repealed the Rumford Act by a margin of nearly two to one (California Secretary of State, 1964) 95 . This overwhelming support for legalizing housing discrimination occurred just one year after the passage of fair housing legislation, demonstrating that legal progress did not reflect genuine acceptance of residential integration.

The California Supreme Court's 1966 ruling that Proposition 14 violated the Fourteenth Amendment restored fair housing protections, but the intervening period allowed discriminatory practices to solidify and become more sophisticated (Reitman v. Mulkey, 1966) 96 . Rather than abandon discrimination, housing providers learned to accomplish the same exclusionary goals through methods that appeared race-neutral but had disparate racial impacts.

Contemporary Discrimination in California Housing

The most recent data from 2024-2025 demonstrates that housing discrimination in California has not disappeared but has evolved into forms that are both more subtle and, in some ways, more pervasive than historical practices. The California Civil Rights Department's comprehensive testing program provides unprecedented insight into how discrimination operates in contemporary housing markets.

The testing results from Los Angeles County and Ventura County reveal discrimination patterns that directly connect to historical exclusion practices. When 54% of tested properties discriminated based on source of income, particularly against Section 8 housing voucher holders, they were effectively continuing the historical practice of economic exclusion that has always accompanied racial discrimination (California Civil Rights Department, 2025) 104 .

Since African American families are disproportionately likely to use housing assistance programs, source-of-income discrimination functions as a proxy for racial discrimination while appearing economically neutral.

The 22% rate of explicit racial discrimination against Black applicants demonstrates that overt bias persists alongside more subtle forms. Testing revealed that Black applicants faced different credit score requirements, higher rental amounts, and differential treatment in ways that directly parallel the exclusionary practices of earlier eras (California Civil Rights Department, 2025). The continuity between historical and contemporary discrimination suggests that exclusionary practices have adapted to legal constraints rather than disappeared.

Familial status discrimination, found in 26% of tested properties, continues historical patterns of limiting Black family formation and stability. When housing providers refuse to offer promotional rates to families with children or attempt to charge higher rents, they replicate the historical practice of making family formation economically unsustainable for African Americans (California Civil Rights Department, 2025)

The Compounding Effects of Historical and Contemporary Barriers

Understanding why California's Black homeownership rate remains so low requires recognizing how historical exclusion created cumulative disadvantages that contemporary discrimination continues to reinforce. The wealth that Sandy Jones, Robert, and Carter Perkins accumulated in 1851-1852 represented the kind of capital formation that, if allowed to continue and compound over generations, could have created the foundation for widespread African American homeownership in California.

Instead, the systematic exclusion that began with their deportation and continued through decades of legal and extra-legal discrimination prevented African American families from accumulating the intergenerational wealth that makes homeownership accessible. Current Federal Reserve data shows that the median white family in California holds wealth of approximately $355,000 compared to $40,900 for Black families—a ratio of nearly 9 to 1 that directly reflects generations of exclusion from wealth-building opportunities (Federal Reserve Bank of San Francisco, 2024

This wealth gap translates directly into homeownership barriers that persist even when overt discrimination is prohibited. When Black families lack the resources for substantial down payments, they become vulnerable to predatory lending practices. When they cannot afford homes in well-resourced neighborhoods, their children attend schools with fewer opportunities, limiting their future earning potential. When they face discrimination in employment and housing simultaneously, their ability to build the credit history and savings necessary for homeownership becomes severely constrained.

The cyclical nature of these barriers explains why legal prohibition of discrimination has not eliminated the homeownership gap. Contemporary discrimination operates against families who start from positions of severe disadvantage created by historical exclusion, making even small acts of bias more consequential than they might appear in isolation.

Current Market Conditions and Their Disparate Impact

California's contemporary housing market conditions create additional barriers that disproportionately affect African American potential homebuyers who are still recovering from generations of exclusion. The median home price in California reached $873,000 in 2024, requiring an annual income of approximately $200,000 to qualify for a traditional mortgage with a 20% down payment (California Association of Realtors, 2024.

These price levels place homeownership beyond the reach of most California families, but they affect African American families most severely because of lower average incomes and accumulated wealth. While 35% of white California households earn over $100,000 annually, only 20% of Black households reach this income level (California Department of Finance, 2024). More significantly, the down payment requirements for California homes—typically $150,000-200,000—exceed the total wealth holdings of most Black families in the state.

Recent data shows that only 8% of Black renter households have at least $20,000 in savings available for down payment assistance, compared to 18% of white renters (Urban Institute, 2024) 100 . This savings gap reflects both lower incomes and the ongoing effects of discrimination in employment, lending, and wealth accumulation that compound over time.

Interest rate increases in 2023-2024 have created additional barriers that disproportionately affect African American homebuyers. When mortgage rates rose from historic lows near 3% to over 7%, the number of Black families who could qualify for median-priced homes dropped by 43% compared to 35% for white families (National Association of Realtors, 2024) 101 . This disparate impact occurs because Black families typically have less wealth to offset higher monthly payments and may depend more heavily on programs that become less attractive at higher interest rates.# Where We Will Start

The Power Is Now Media Inc. is based in Riverside, California, positioning us at the epicenter of one of America's most complex and troubling homeownership stories. When we examine where to begin our African American Homeownership Initiative, California provides both the most urgent need and the most instructive example of how historical discrimination creates persistent contemporary barriers. California's Black homeownership rate today stands at approximately 38-41% compared to nearly 70% for white families—a gap that is not only wider than the national average but represents a rate lower now than it was in the 1960s when it was completely legal to discriminate against Black homebuyers (California Housing Finance Agency, 2024)

This stark reality demands our immediate attention and action. The latest data from 2024-2025 reveals that California's housing discrimination persists in forms both overt and subtle, with the California Civil Rights Department conducting over 120 phone tests and nearly 100 in-person tests across Los Angeles County and Ventura County in 2024 alone (California Civil Rights Department, 2025) 104 . The results paint a disturbing picture: 54% of tested properties demonstrated discrimination based on source of income, 22% showed racial discrimination against Black applicants, 26% discriminated against families with children, and 23% discriminated based on disability (California Civil Rights Department, 2025.

Understanding why California's African American homeownership rate remains so devastatingly low requires examining how the state's history of systematic exclusion continues to reverberate through contemporary housing markets. California's history of housing discrimination against African Americans represents one of the most comprehensive and deliberate exclusion campaigns in American history, beginning with the state's first governor and continuing through sophisticated modern practices that maintain racial segregation while appearing race-neutral.

The Power to Start and The Power to Stop: Contemporary Application

Drawing from the historical analysis and current conditions, our initiative recognizes that addressing California's homeownership disparities requires both starting new approaches and stopping practices that perpetuate exclusion. The "Power to Start and Power to Stop" framework applies directly to contemporary conditions while acknowledging the historical roots of current disparities.

The Power to Start Knowledge

takes on new urgency when we recognize that African American families in California face discrimination patterns that have evolved over 175 years but maintain consistent exclusionary purposes. Knowledge must include not only financial literacy and homebuying processes but also understanding of legal rights, recognition of discriminatory practices, and awareness of available resources and protections

Recent innovations in homebuyer education demonstrate the potential for targeted knowledge transfer. The California Housing Finance Agency's Building Black Wealth program has served over 9,000 families with $165 million in down payment assistance, focusing specifically on counties with significant African American populations (California Housing Finance Agency, 2024) 48 . This targeted approach acknowledges that generic homebuyer education has proven insufficient to address the specific barriers African American families face.

Current market conditions in California make this belief particularly challenging to sustain. When median home prices require incomes that exceed what most families earn, and when discrimination testing reveals ongoing bias in over half of housing transactions, optimism about homeownership must be grounded in realistic strategies rather than wishful thinking.

Starting to act instead of procrastinating applies to both individuals and systems. For families, action means beginning financial preparation even when homeownership seems distant. For institutions, action means implementing targeted programs that address specific barriers rather than hoping that general economic growth will eventually create equity.

The success of Special Purpose Credit Programs demonstrates how institutional action can create new pathways to homeownership.

These programs, now explicitly authorized by federal regulators, allow lenders to offer flexible terms specifically to address historical exclusion of minority borrowers (Office of the Comptroller of the Currency, 2024) 102 . Early results show approval rates for qualified Black applicants that approach those of white applicants, suggesting that institutional changes can overcome barriers that individual preparation alone cannot address.

Commitment to financial independence requires recognition that traditional paths to wealth building have been systematically closed to African American families in California. Financial independence must be pursued through available means while working to expand access to wealth-building opportunities that have historically been restricted.

This commitment extends beyond individual family financial management to include advocacy for policy changes that address structural barriers. When housing discrimination persists at rates documented by current testing, individual financial preparation must be combined with collective action to address discriminatory practices.

Starting to live within your means and not for others takes on particular significance in California's high-cost environment. The pressure to maintain appearances in expensive markets can undermine the long-term savings necessary for homeownership, but this pressure must be balanced against the reality that delayed homeownership becomes increasingly expensive over time as home prices typically appreciate faster than wages.

Living on a budget and creating a plan becomes essential when homeownership requires substantial capital accumulation in high-cost markets. Modern budgeting tools and apps provide capabilities that were unavailable to previous generations, but the fundamental discipline required remains constant.

Saving money for emergencies assumes greater importance when homeownership represents a larger portion of family wealth and when discrimination may limit access to traditional forms of credit during financial difficulties. Emergency funds must account for both typical homeownership costs and the additional expenses that may result from discrimination in employment or other areas.

Paying off credit card debt directly addresses one of the key barriers identified in contemporary mortgage denials. Black mortgage applicants have average debt-to-income ratios of 40% compared to 33% for white applicants, partly due to higher reliance on credit for expenses that other families might cover with accumulated wealth (Consumer Financial Protection Bureau, 2024).

Working on restoring and maintaining credit scores addresses the documented disparity in credit access and treatment that continues to affect African American borrowers. The median credit score for Black mortgage applicants of 629 compared to approximately 729 for white applicants reflects both individual credit management challenges and systematic barriers to credit access that compound over time (Consumer Financial Protection Bureau, 2024).

The Power to Stop: Ending Practices That Perpetuate Disparities

The "Power to Stop" framework addresses both individual behaviors that limit wealth accumulation and systematic practices that maintain exclusion. Understanding how historical discrimination evolved into contemporary barriers helps identify which practices must be stopped to create genuine opportunity for homeownership equity.

Stopping indiscriminate spending becomes crucial when homeownership requires substantial capital accumulation in markets where median homes cost $873,000. However, this individual responsibility must be balanced against recognition that spending discipline alone cannot overcome systematic barriers that limit income and wealth accumulation opportunities.

Stopping daily dining out, financing clothes and shoes, financing cars and vacations represents traditional financial discipline advice that applies to all families seeking homeownership.

In California's expensive markets, these savings become even more important because the amounts needed for down payments and closing costs exceed what many families earn in entire years.

Stopping all auto-pays and unnecessary memberships provides immediate budget relief that can be redirected toward homeownership goals. These practices become particularly important when saving for homeownership requires sustained discipline over multiple years.

Stopping excuses and complaints requires acknowledging both individual responsibility and systematic barriers. While individuals must take responsibility for their financial decisions and preparation, systemic discrimination documented by contemporary testing results demands collective action rather than individual acceptance.

Stopping hope without strategy emphasizes the need for concrete action plans that account for both current market realities and available resources. Hope must be grounded in realistic assessment of barriers and identification of specific pathways to overcome them.

California as a Laboratory for National Solutions

California's experience with homeownership discrimination provides both cautionary lessons and innovative solutions that can inform national approaches to closing racial homeownership gaps. The state's comprehensive fair housing testing program, targeted down payment assistance, and Special Purpose Credit Programs offer models for addressing persistent discrimination while creating new pathways to homeownership.

The California Civil Rights Department's enforcement approach, which combines proactive testing with targeted education and systematic policy changes, demonstrates how state agencies can address discrimination more effectively than federal enforcement alone (California Civil Rights Department, 2025) 104 . Their issuance of 758 compliance notices in 2024, including 374 addressing fair housing violations, shows the scale of intervention necessary to address contemporary discrimination.

Similarly, the California Housing Finance Agency's Building Black Wealth initiative demonstrates how targeted programs can achieve results that generic homeownership promotion cannot accomplish. By focusing specifically on barriers affecting African American families and providing both down payment assistance and culturally relevant education, the program has served thousands of families who would not have achieved homeownership through traditional means (California Housing Finance Agency, 2024).

Our African American Homeownership Initiative builds upon these California innovations while addressing the specific needs of communities we serve. By starting in Riverside, California, where both historical discrimination and contemporary barriers are well-documented, we can develop approaches that address the full range of obstacles that maintain homeownership disparities. The lessons learned in California can then inform expansion to other markets where similar patterns of historical exclusion continue to limit African American homeownership today.

The historical analysis reveals that California's current homeownership disparities are not accidents or natural market outcomes but the predictable result of systematic exclusion that began with the state's founding and continues through contemporary discrimination. Addressing these disparities requires interventions that are as systematic and sustained as the discrimination they seek to overcome. The Power Is Now Media's initiative represents our commitment to developing and implementing such comprehensive approaches, starting where the need is greatest and the lessons learned can benefit African American communities nationwide.

ABOUT THE AUTHOR

Mr. Eric Lawrence Frazier, MBA
President & CEO, The Power Is Now Media

Mr. Eric Lawrence Frazier, MBA, is the President and CEO of The Power Is Now Media, a national multimedia company dedicated to real estate education, empowerment, and thought leadership. Through its expansive platform—The Power Is Now website (www.thepowerisnow.com), national podcast networks, social media channels, and live-stream television platforms—the company delivers timely, authoritative content on real estate, lending, economics, and government policy.

Publishing and Educational Contributions

As Publisher and Editor-in-Chief of The Power Is Now Publishing, Mr. Frazier oversees the production of books and magazines focused on real estate, financial literacy, and wealth building. Since its founding, the publishing division has developed The Power Is Now Magazines—a suite of online real estate publications launched in 2013 that offer market insights, national news, and educational resources for homebuyers and professionals.

Academic Background

Mr. Frazier holds both a Master of Business Administration (MBA) with an emphasis in Finance and a Bachelor of Science in Business Administration and Management from the University of Redlands, California.
He has lectured on the U.S. mortgage crisis at the University of California, Riverside, addressing international business leaders from India, and has also served as an adjunct professor.

Professional Expertise and Experience

With over four decades of experience in mortgage banking, Mr. Frazier is recognized nationally for his leadership in origination, underwriting, operations, management, and marketing.
He also holds a California real estate license for over thirty years and a broker's license (#01143484) for more than twenty-eight years.
Together with his wife, he founded Frazier Group Realty (www.fraziergrouprealty.com), a full-service, family-owned real estate company based in Riverside, California.

Spiritual Leadership

Mr. Frazier serves as a pastor and leads The Power Is Now Ministries, part of the North Fontana Church, a registered 501(c) nonprofit organization.
Through this ministry, he continues his mission of teaching, outreach, and mentorship.

Industry Leadership and Associations

Mr. Frazier's leadership extends across multiple professional associations. He has served as:

- President, Orange County Realtist chapter of the National Association of Real Estate Brokers (NAREB)
- Director, California Association of Real Estate Brokers
- Vice President, Orange County chapter of the National Association of Hispanic Real Estate Professionals (NAHREP)
- Advisory Board Member, Orange County chapter of the Asian Real Estate Association of America (AREAA)
- Board Member, Riverside Fair Housing Council
- He is also a current member of the Inland Valley Association of Realtors (IVAR).

Civic and Community Leadership

Beyond real estate, Mr. Frazier is committed to community service and education.

He has served on the Board of Directors of Project Tomorrow (www.tomorrow.org), a national nonprofit focused on advancing education.

He is an active member of:

- 100 Black Men of America
- NAACP
- National Association of Mortgage Brokers
- He is also a past President and Director of the State of California African American Museum (www.caamuseum.org).

Connect with Mr. Frazier

All of Mr. Frazier's professional work, publications, and affiliations can be found on his LinkedIn profile:
👉 www.linkedin.com/in/ericfrazier

Author, Speaker, and Creative Leader

A man of many talents, Mr. Frazier is also an author, blogger, poet, singer, songwriter, motivational speaker, business consultant, and coach for both for-profit and nonprofit organizations.

He has published six books on poetry, African American wealth, credit, and business.

His personal interests include golf, running, and jazz music.

Mentorship and Family Life

Mr. Frazier is deeply passionate about mentorship, serving as a role model for African American men and offering guidance to young people and adults alike.

His greatest joy is family—he has been married to Ruby, the love of his life, for over forty years. Together they have raised four accomplished daughters:

- Three hold master's degrees in management and business
- The youngest holds a bachelor's degree in apparel merchandising and management

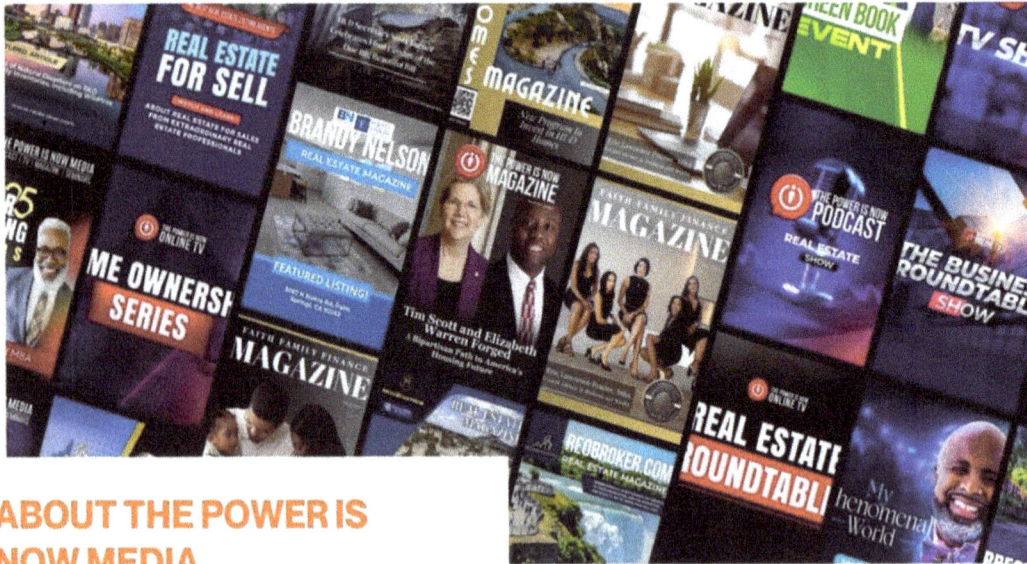

ABOUT THE POWER IS NOW MEDIA

Founded in 2009 by Eric L. Frazier, MBA, The Power Is Now Media is an online multimedia company headquartered in Riverside, California.

We are passionate advocates for homeownership, wealth building, and financial literacy.

Through our diverse platforms—including nationally syndicated radio, podcasts, magazines, TV, social media, streaming platforms, and live online seminars and webinars—we create and publish original educational content about real estate and financial empowerment.

As a trusted online platform and learning resource, we provide valuable information about homeownership, housing programs, loan options, and down payment assistance to help individuals and families achieve financial literacy and the American Dream of homeownership.

We are proudly supported by housing finance agencies, real estate associations, and civic, religious, and community organizations, helping them amplify their voice and promote their services and programs in lending, housing, and homeownership.

Visit us online: www.thepowerisnow.com

Our Mission

The mission of The Power Is Now Media is to inspire and educate both consumers and real estate professionals to build wealth through real estate—from acquisition and management to sale.

We achieve this through our website, live and on-demand TV, and social media platforms, providing trusted information and tools that empower everyone to own real estate now and attain the American Dream of homeownership.

Company Slogan:

"We are leading the conversation about homeownership."

Address:
3739 6th Street, Riverside, CA 92501

Telephone/Fax:
800-401-8994

Founder & CEO:
Eric Lawrence Frazier, MBA

- California Licensed Loan Originator (NMLS License #461807)
- California Real Estate Broker (License #01148434)

WHY BECOME A MEMBER OF THE POWER IS NOW MEDIA?

Unlock exclusive access to the most powerful real estate, mortgage, credit, and wealth-building content in the industry.

For a limited time, become a member for only $10/month or $60/year. Your membership delivers undeniable value, insider access, and proven tools to help you buy, sell, invest, and build wealth with confidence.

Membership Benefits

Exclusive Streaming & Shows

· Unlimited access to The Power Is Now TV Network library of hundreds of shows, podcasts, and webinars.
· Daily programming on homeownership, real estate investing, mortgages, credit, and financial literacy.
· Member-only live streams and roundtable discussions with top industry leaders.

Free Digital Resources

- Real estate eBooks, guides, and reports on buying, selling, investing, and credit strategies.
- Buyer & Seller Guides, HUD Homes Guide, and Foreclosure Market Reports, updated quarterly.
- Access to The Power Is Now Media Resource Library of downloadable content.

Magazines & Newsletters

- Complimentary subscription to The Power Is Now National Real Estate Magazine.
- Complimentary subscription to The Power Is Now HUD Homes for Sale Magazine.
- Complimentary subscription to The Power Is Now TV Guide Magazine.
- Complimentary subscription to Faith, Family & Finance Magazine.
- Weekly newsletters with videos, infographics, and market insights.

THE POWER IS NOW MEDIA

Member Engagement

- Invitations to attend and participate in live recordings of the Real Estate Roundtable and Business Roundtable.
- Networking opportunities with agents, lenders, investors, and entrepreneurs nationwide.
- Priority access to quarterly webinars for first-time homebuyers, investors, and asset managers.
- Monthly group coaching sessions on Personal Finance, Real Estate, Mortgage, and Media.

Discounts & Savings

- Member-only discounts on media services (podcast hosting, YouTube TV production, private-label magazines, website redesigns, social media management).
- Exclusive pricing on advertising, sponsorships, and coaching programs.

Community & Recognition

- Become part of a national network of professionals and consumers committed to real estate wealth-building.
- Opportunities to feature your story, listings, or business on The Power Is Now TV Network.
- Special Membership Offer

Special Launch Price: $10/month or $60/year (limited-time offer through year-end).
Regular Price: $50/month or $325/year. Don't wait—membership pays for itself many times over.

References

1. National Association of Realtors. "2024 Profileof HomeBuyersandSellersHighlights." November 2024.
https://www.nar.realtor/sites/default/files/2024-11/2024-profile-of-home-buyers-and-sellers-highlights-11-04-2024_2.pdf.
2. TIAA Institute-GFLEC. "The TIAA Institute-GFLEC Personal Finance Index (P-Fin Index)." 2024.
https://gflec.org/wp-content/uploads/2024/04/TIAA_GFLEC_Report_PFin_April2024_07.pdf.
3. Federal Reserve. "Greater Wealth, Greater Uncertainty: Changes in Racial Inequality in the Survey of Consumer Finances." October 18, 2023.
https://www.federalreserve.gov/econres/notes/feds-notes/greater-wealth-greater-uncertainty-changes-in-racial-inequality-in-the-survey-of-consumer-finances-20231018.html.
4. Annuity.org. "Financial Literacy & African Americans: Bridging the Gap." 2024.
https://www.annuity.org/financial-literacy/black-community/.
5. Economic Policy Institute. "Strong Wage Growth for Low-Wage Workers Bucks the Historic Trend." 2024.
https://www.epi.org/publication/strong-wage-growth-for-low-wage-workers-bucks-the-historic-trend/.
6. Governing. "California Has a Huge Wage Gap by Race and Gender." 2024.
https://www.governing.com/work/california-has-a-huge-wage-gap-by-race-and-gender.
7. Fresnoland. "Black, Latino Californians Face Greatest Barriers to Homeownership." May 6, 2024.
https://fresnoland.org/2024/05/06/black-and-latino-californians-face-the-greatest-barriers-to-homeownership-new-study-says-thats-almost-60-of-fresno/.
8. Consumer Financial Protection Bureau. "Summary of 2023 Data on Mortgage Lending." 2024.
https://www.consumerfinance.gov/data-research/hmda/summary-of-2023-data-on-mortgage-lending/.
9. Federal Reserve Bank of Minneapolis. "Lender-Reported Reasons for Mortgage Denials Don't Explain Racial Disparities." 2024.
https://www.minneapolisfed.org/article/2024/lender-reported-reasons-for-mortgage-denials-dont-explain-racial-disparities.
10. Consumer Financial Protection Bureau. "Summary of 2022 Data on Mortgage Lending." 2023.
https://www.consumerfinance.gov/data-research/hmda/summary-of-2022-data-on-mortgage-lending/.
11. PubMed Central. "Racial/Ethnic Inequality & Contemporary Disparities in Mortgage Lending." 2024.
https://pmc.ncbi.nlm.nih.gov/articles/PMC11731762/.
12. National Association of Realtors. "2023 Snapshot of Race and Home Buying in America." March 2, 2023.
https://www.nar.realtor/sites/default/files/documents/2023-snapshot-of-race-and-home-buying-in-the-us-03-02-2023.pdf.
13. HUD User. "Long-Term Impact Report: The HUD First-Time Homebuyer Education and Counseling Demonstration." 2024.
https://www.huduser.gov/portal/publications/Long-Term-Impact-Report-HUD-First-Time-Homebuyer-Education-Counseling-Demonstration.html.
14. California Housing Finance Agency. "CalHFA Launches Building Black Wealth Initiative to Address Homeownership Gap." February 9, 2021. https://www.calhfa.ca.gov/about/press/press-releases/2021/pr2021-02-09.htm.
15. CalMatters. "What California Lawmakers Could Do to Boost Homeownership for Black Families." May 2021.
https://calmatters.org/housing/2021/05/california-homeownership-black/.
16. GroundBreak Coalition. "Advancing Black Homeownership through Partnership, Innovation, and Scale." June 7, 2024.
https://groundbreakcoalition.org/news-updates/advancing-black-homeownership-through-partnership-innovation-and-scale/.
17. Twin Cities Habitat for Humanity. "Advancing Black Homeownership Program Sees Impactful Results." 2024.
https://www.tchabitat.org/blog/advancing-black-homeownership-program-results.
18. California Housing Finance Agency. "Black Homeownership Initiative: Building Black Wealth." 2024.
https://www.calhfa.ca.gov/community/buildingblackwealth.htm.
19. National Fair Housing Alliance. "2024 Fair Housing Trends Report." July 30, 2024.
https://nationalfairhousing.org/resource/2024-fair-housing-trends-report/.
20. U.S. Department of Housing and Urban Development. "HUD Announces More Than $22 Million to Combat Housing Discrimination in America." October 1, 2024. https://www.hud.gov/press/press_releases_media_advisories/HUD_No_24_259.
21. Center on Budget and Policy Priorities. "Administration's Recent Actions Severely Weaken Protections and Eliminate Resources for People Facing Housing Discrimination." July 2, 2025.
https://www.cbpp.org/blog/administrations-recent-actions-severely-weaken-protections-and-eliminate-resources-for-people.
22. HUD User. "Combating Housing Discrimination To Build Inclusive Communities." 2024.
https://www.huduser.gov/portal/pdredge/pdr_edge_featd_article_081114.html.
23. Urban Institute. "How the Fair Housing Act's Role in Combating Discrimination Will Continue to Evolve." May 2, 2018.
https://www.urban.org/urban-wire/how-fair-housing-acts-role-combating-discrimination-will-continue-evolve.
24. Fannie Mae. "HomeView Homebuyer Education." 2025. https://www.fanniemae.com/education.
25. Framework Homeownership. "Framework Homebuyer Education Course." April 24, 2025.
https://frameworkhomeownership.org/get-started/.
26. U.S. Department of the Treasury. "Homeowner Assistance Fund." July 21, 2025.
https://home.treasury.gov/policy-issues/coronavirus/assistance-for-state-local-and-tribal-governments/homeowner-assistance-fund.
27. National Association of Real Estate Brokers. "Two Million New Black Homeowners Program (2Mn5)." September 12, 2019.
https://www.nareb.com/2mn5/.
28. Bankrate. "The State Of Black Homeownership In 2025." February 13, 2025.
https://www.bankrate.com/homeownership/black-homeownership-today/.
29. Ballard Brief. "The Homeownership Gap between Black and White Families in the United States." January 2, 2025.
https://ballardbrief.byu.edu/issue-briefs/the-homeownership-gap-between-black-and-white-families-in-the-united-states.

30. National Association of Realtors. "Racial Minority Groups Increased Their Homeownership Rates While Still Facing Significant Homebuying Challenges." February 20, 2024. https://www.nar.realtor/newsroom/racial-minority-groups-increased-their-homeownership-rates-while-still-facing-significant-homeb uying-challenges.
31. CNN Business. "Homeownership Gap Between Black and White Owners Is Worse Now Than a Decade Ago." February 20, 2024. https://www.cnn.com/2024/02/20/economy/black-white-homeownership-gap/index.html.
32. Urban Institute. "Black Homeownership Increased Slightly during the Pandemic, but High Interest Rates Threaten to Further Widen Racial Homeownership Gaps." April 8, 2025. https://www.urban.org/urban-wire/black-homeownership-increased-slightly-during-pandemic-high-interest-rates-threaten.
33. U.S. Department of the Treasury. "Racial Differences in Economic Security: Housing." December 6, 2022. https://home.treasury.gov/news/featured-stories/racial-differences-in-economic-security-housing.
34. HUD User. "Closing the African American Homeownership Gap." 2021. https://www.huduser.gov/portal/pdredge/pdr-edge-featd-article-032221.html.
35. Eye on Housing. "Homeownership Rates by Race and Ethnicity." February 6, 2024. https://eyeonhousing.org/2024/02/homeownership-rates-by-race-and-ethnicity-3/.
36. Urban Institute. "Mapping the Black Homeownership Gap." February 26, 2018. https://www.urban.org/urban-wire/mapping-black-homeownership-gap.
37. Othering & Belonging Institute. "Racial Disparities in California's Homeownership Rates." 2024. https://belonging.berkeley.edu/racial-disparities-californias-homeownership-rates.
38. HousingWire. "NAR: Black Homeownership Growth Challenges 2025." March 15, 2025. https://www.housingwire.com/articles/nar-black-homeownership-growth-challenges-2025/.
39. LendingTree. "Black Americans Own Disproportionately Small Share of Homes in 50 Largest US Metros." February 3, 2025. https://www.lendingtree.com/home/mortgage/black-americans-homeownership-trends/.
40. U.S. Census Bureau. "Households With a White, Non-Hispanic Householder Were Ten Times Wealthier Than Those With a Black Householder in 2021." 2024. https://www.census.gov/library/stories/2024/04/wealth-by-race.html.
41. Survey of Income and Program Participation. Referenced in U.S. Census Bureau analysis, 2022.
42. National League of Cities. "Housing for Black-Led Households." February 6, 2024. https://www.nlc.org/article/2024/02/06/housing-for-black-led-households/.
43. California Association of Realtors. "2024 Housing Affordability by Ethnicity." 2025. https://www.car.org/aboutus/mediacenter/newsreleases/2025releases/2024haibyethnicity.
44. California Legislative Analyst's Office. "California Housing Affordability Tracker (2nd Quarter 2025)." 2025. https://lao.ca.gov/LAOEconTax/Article/Detail/793.
45. PRNewswire. "Homeownership Slips Further Out of Reach for All California Ethnic Groups Amid Rising Mortgage Costs, C.A.R. Reports." April 24, 2025. https://www.prnewswire.com/news-releases/homeownership-slips-further-out-of-reach-for-all-california-ethnic-groups-amid-rising-mortgage-costs-car-reports-302437521.html.
46. Governor of California. "Governor Newsom Signs Into Law Groundbreaking Reforms to Build More Housing, Boost Affordability." July 11, 2025. https://www.gov.ca.gov/2025/06/30/governor-newsom-signs-into-law-groundbreaking-reforms-to-build-more-housing-affordability/ .
47. CalMatters. "Californians: Here's Why Your Housing Costs Are So High." January 16, 2025. https://calmatters.org/explainers/california-housing-costs-explainer/.
48. National Association of Realtors. "Black Homeownership Rate Sees Largest Annual Increase Among Racial Groups but Still Trails White Homeownership Rate by Almost 30 Percentage Points." March 17, 2025. https://www.nar.realtor/newsroom/black-homeownership-rate-sees-largest-annual-increase-among-racial-groups-but-still-trails-whit e-homeownership-rate.
49. U.S. Census Bureau. "Rate of Homeownership Higher Than Before Pandemic in All Regions." December 8, 2022. https://www.census.gov/library/stories/2023/07/younger-householders-drove-rebound-in-homeownership.html.
50. National Association of Hispanic Real Estate Professionals. "State of Hispanic Homeownership Report." April 4, 2019. https://nahrep.org/shhr/.
51. Local Housing Solutions. "Recent Homeownership Trends Among Households of Color." September 18, 2024. https://localhousingsolutions.org/lab/notes/recent-homeownership-trends-among-households-of-color/.
52. Urban Institute. "Black Homeownership Gap: Research Trends and Why the Growing Gap Matters." June 20, 2019. https://www.urban.org/events/black-homeownership-gap-research-trends-and-why-growing-gap-matters.
53. National Association of Home Builders. "Nearly 60% of U.S. Households Unable to Afford a $300K Home." March 2025. https://www.nahb.org/blog/2025/03/priced-out-affordability-pyramid.
54. National Association of Home Builders. "Income Growth Helps Mute Existing Affordability Constraints." May 2025. https://www.nahb.org/news-and-economics/press-releases/2025/05/income-growth-helps-mute-existing-affordability-constraints.
55. U.S. Census Bureau. "Nearly Half of Renter Households Are Cost-Burdened, Proportions Differ by Race." September 12, 2024. https://www.census.gov/newsroom/press-releases/2024/renter-households-cost-burdened-race.html.
56. Statista. "House-price-to-income Ratio in Selected Countries 2024." 2024. https://www.statista.com/statistics/237529/price-to-income-ratio-of-housing-worldwide/.
57. Mortgage Professional. "Black Americans Still Face Higher Mortgage Denial Rates, Study Finds." July 15, 2025. https://www.mpamag.com/us/mortgage-industry/industry-trends/black-americans-still-face-higher-mortgage-denial-rates-study-find s/542601.

58. Newsweek. "Black Homeownership is Set to Soar." February 21, 2024.
   https://www.newsweek.com/black-home-ownership-set-soar-1871585.
59. Scotsman Guide. "Mortgage Denial Rates Are Nearly Double for Black Applicants: LendingTree." July 11, 2025.
   https://www.scotsmanguide.com/news/mortgage-denial-rates-are-nearly-double-for-black-applicants/.
60. LendingTree. "Black Homebuyers 1.7 Times More Likely to Be Denied for Mortgages Than All Homebuyers." July 7, 2020.
   https://www.lendingtree.com/home/mortgage/lendingtree-study-black-homebuyers-more-likely-to-be-denied-mortgages-than-other-homebuyers/.
61. National Community Reinvestment Coalition. "60% Black Homeownership: A Radical Goal for Black Wealth Development." October
   13, 2021. https://ncrc.org/60-black-homeownership-a-radical-goal-for-black-wealth-development/.
62. National Association of Realtors. "Home Buyers and Sellers Generational Trends." April 3, 2024.
   https://www.nar.realtor/research-and-statistics/research-reports/home-buyer-and-seller-generational-trends.
63. Krimmel, Jake, Sabrina Speianu, and Danielle Hale. "June 2025 Monthly Housing Market Trends Report." Realtor.com Research,
   Realtor.com, July 8, 2025. https://www.realtor.com/research/june-2025-data/
64. Freddie Mac. "Economic, Housing and Mortgage Market Outlook – November 2024 | Spotlight: Housing Supply." November 2024.
   https://www.freddiemac.com/research/forecast/20241126-us-economy-remains-resilient-with-strong-q3-growth.
65. Xu, Jiayi, and Danielle Hale. "While Black Homeownership Gaps Still Exist, Female and Millennials Are the Key Driver of Black
   Homeownership." Realtor.com Economic Research, Realtor.com, February 9, 2022.
   https://www.realtor.com/research/black-recent-homebuyers-2022/
66. U.S. News. "2025-2030 Five-Year Housing Market Predictions." July 9, 2025.
   https://realestate.usnews.com/real-estate/housing-market-index/articles/housing-market-predictions-for-the-next-5-years.
67. Black Economic Alliance. "Homepage - Black Economic Alliance." June 20, 2025. https://blackeconomicalliance.org/.
68. Black Economic Alliance Foundation. "Black Economic Alliance Foundation Unveils 'Architecture For Action' to Drive Black Economic
   Prosperity." May 29, 2024.
   https://blackeconomicalliance.org/press-release/black-economic-alliance-foundation-unveils-architecture-for-action-to-drive-black-economic-prosperity/.
69. NAREB Convention. "NAREB National Convention." 2024. https://narebconvention.com/.
70. NAREB Building Black Wealth Tour. "NAREB Building Black Wealth Tour." 2025. https://narebblackwealthtour.com/.
71. Houston Style Magazine. "NAREB's 2025 Mid-Winter Conference: Elevating Black Homeownership & Real Estate Excellence."
   February 7, 2025.
   https://stylemagazine.com/news/2025/feb/07/narebs-2025-mid-winter-conference-elevating-black-homeownership-real-estate-excellence/.
72. The Washington Post. "The 'heartbreaking' decrease in black homeownership." February 28, 2019.
   https://www.washingtonpost.com/news/business/wp/2019/02/28/feature/the-heartbreaking-decrease-in-black-homeownership/.
73. Urban Institute. "A closer look at the fifteen-year drop in black homeownership." February 12, 2018.
   https://www.urban.org/urban-wire/closer-look-fifteen-year-drop-black-homeownership.
74. Population Reference Bureau. "U.S. Homeownership Rates Fall Among Young Adults, African Americans." 2024.
   https://www.prb.org/resources/u-s-homeownership-rates-fall-among-young-adults-african-americans/.
75. Statista. "Rate of homeownership in the United States in 2023, by race." March 1, 2024.
   https://www.statista.com/statistics/639685/us-home-ownership-rate-by-race/.
76. National Association of Realtors. "2024 Snapshot of Race and Home Buying in America." February 20, 2024.
   https://www.nar.realtor/sites/default/files/documents/2024-snapshot-of-race-and-home-buying-in-america-02-20-2024.pdf.
77. Urban Institute. "These Five Facts Reveal the Current Crisis in Black Homeownership." July 31, 2019.
   https://www.urban.org/urban-wire/these-five-facts-reveal-current-crisis-black-homeownership.
78. Education Data. "Student Loan Debt by Race [2024]: Analysis of Statistics." February 19, 2025.
   https://educationdata.org/student-loan-debt-by-race.
79. The Pew Charitable Trusts. "The Student Loan Default Divide: Racial Inequities Play a Role." April 4, 2025.
   https://www.pew.org/en/research-and-analysis/reports/2024/12/the-student-loan-default-divide-racial-inequities-play-a-role.
80. National Association of Realtors. "Race, Homeownership, and Student Loan Debt." October 5, 2021.
   https://www.nar.realtor/blogs/economists-outlook/race-homeownership-and-student-loan-debt.
81. National Community Reinvestment Coalition. "A First Look at the Intersection of Mortgage Lending and Race in 2024." April 3, 2025.
   https://ncrc.org/a-first-look-at-the-intersection-of-mortgage-lending-and-race-in-2024/.
82. Joint Center for Housing Studies. "High-Income Black Homeowners Receive Higher Interest Rates than Low-Income White
   Homeowners." 2024.
   https://www.jchs.harvard.edu/blog/high-income-black-homeowners-receive-higher-interest-rates-low-income-white-homeowners.
83. THE CITY. "Black Home Mortgage Borrowers Pay More in NYC, New Study Finds." October 22, 2024.
   https://www.thecity.nyc/2024/10/22/black-home-mortgage-borrowers/.
84. CBS News. "Mortgage discrimination: Black and Latino paying millions more in interest, study shows." November 15, 2019.
   https://www.cbsnews.com/news/mortgage-discrimination-black-and-latino-paying-millions-more-in-interest-study-shows/.
85. Financial Samurai. "Mortgage Interest Rates By Race: The Differences Are Significant." April 1, 2025.
   https://www.financialsamurai.com/mortgage-interest-rates-by-race/.
86. Urban Institute. "What Different Denial Rates Can Tell Us About Racial Disparities in the Mortgage Market." April 2, 2025.
   https://www.urban.org/urban-wire/what-different-denial-rates-can-tell-us-about-racial-disparities-mortgage-market.
87. Housing Matters. "How Student Loan Debt Affects the Racial Homeownership Gap." September 14, 2022.
   https://housingmatters.urban.org/articles/how-student-loan-debt-affects-racial-homeownership-gap.
88. Urban Institute. "Student Loan Debt and Access to Homeownership for Borrowers of Color." November 7, 2022.
   https://www.urban.org/research/publication/student-loan-debt-and-access-homeownership-borrowers-color.

89. California Civil Rights Department. "During Fair Housing Month, Civil Rights Department Shares New Data on Housing Discrimination in Southern California." April 17, 2025. https://calcivilrights.ca.gov/2025/04/17/during-fair-housing-month-civil-rights-department-shares-new-data-on-housing-discrimination-in-southern-california/.

90. Oregon Historical Society. "Oregon Black Exclusion Laws." 2019. https://www.oregonhistory.org/education/oregon-history-wayfinder/era-2/topic-2/oregon-black-exclusion-laws.htm.

91. Bancroft Library, University of California Berkeley. "California Gold Rush Records." 1885.

92. https://bancroft.berkeley.edu/collections/californiana.html.

93. California State Archives. "Fugitive Slave Cases in California." 1852. https://www.sos.ca.gov/archives/collections/1850s/fugitive-slave-cases. Proceedings of the California Constitutional Convention. "Constitutional Convention Debates." 1849. California State Library Digital Collections.

94. California State Archives. "California Fair Housing Act of 1963 (Rumford Act)." 1963. https://www.sos.ca.gov/archives/collections/1960s/fair-housing-act.

95. California Secretary of State. "Proposition 14 Election Results." 1964. https://www.sos.ca.gov/elections/prior-elections/1964/proposition-14.

96. Reitman v. Mulkey, 387 U.S. 369 (1967). Supreme Court of the United States.

97. Federal Reserve Bank of San Francisco. "Racial Wealth Gap in California." 2024. https://www.frbsf.org/economic-research/publications/economic-letter/2024/june/racial-wealth-gap-california/.

98. California Association of Realtors. "California Housing Market Data." 2024. https://www.car.org/marketdata/data/housingdata.

99. California Department of Finance. "California Household Income by Race and Ethnicity." 2024. https://dof.ca.gov/forecasting/economics/economic-indicators/household-income/.

100. Urban Institute. "Down Payment Challenges for Black Homebuyers." 2024. https://www.urban.org/research/publication/down-payment-challenges-black-homebuyers.

101. National Association of Realtors. "Black Homeownership Rate Sees Largest Annual Increase Among Racial Groups." March 17, 2025. https://www.nar.realtor/newsroom/black-homeownership-rate-sees-largest-annual-increase-among-racial-groups-but-still-trails-white-homeownership-rate.

102. Office of the Comptroller of the Currency. "Special Purpose Credit Programs." 2024. https://www.occ.gov/topics/consumers-and-communities/cra/special-purpose-credit-programs.html.

103. Consumer Financial Protection Bureau. "Summary of 2024 Data on Mortgage Lending." 2024. https://www.consumerfinance.gov/data-research/hmda/summary-of-2024-data-on-mortgage-lending/.

www.ingramcontent.com/pod-product-compliance
Lightning Source LLC
Chambersburg PA
CBHW062050090426
42740CB00016B/3085